Collins

Adheres to National Education Policy
PREPARATORY STAGE

WINDMILLS PLUS

Integrated Semester Course

5 Teacher's Manual

Social Studies

Collins Connect

Series Editor
Padmini Sriraman

Preface

Windmills Plus is an integrated semester course for Classes 1 to 5. The course adheres to the guidelines of the *National Education Policy* (NEP) 2020, and is designed to offer a comprehensive learning package that covers English, Mathematics, Science, Environmental Studies, Social Studies and General Knowledge through 10 Coursebooks and 5 Workbooks.

The course package for each semester consists of a Coursebook and Workbook for the students, and Teacher's Resource book and DigiSuite for the teachers. The books provide ample opportunities to the students to learn, explore and practise new concepts effortlessly across different subjects through an integrated and cross-curricular approach.

Windmills Plus facilitates faster acquisition of knowledge and learning by helping the learners make interdisciplinary connections through cross-curricular links given in the lessons that ensure a rich learning experience. Through a good balance between teacher-led and learner-initiated activities, and the enquiry and skill-based approach, these books help reinforce learning at each level, and contribute to the overall development of the affective and cognitive abilities in students.

Windmills Teacher's Manuals for Social Studies are designed to help the teachers prepare students for the course. This resource book includes detailed Lesson Plans, Answer Keys and Additional Worksheets with answers for all the chapters. The period-wise lesson plans provide the objectives of the lesson, the resources to be used, activities to be done while teaching, and methods to tackle the review exercises and student's assessment. The additional worksheets would facilitate periodic assessment.

Key Features

- Detailed Lesson Plans for all chapters given period-wise
- Suggestions for additional activities for teaching in the lesson plans
- Additional Worksheets to facilitate assessment for each chapter
- Answer keys with answers to all questions in the book
- Answer keys with answers to all additional worksheets
- Answer keys with answers to the workbook

The series is supported by Collins DigiSuite for Teachers that comprises an interactive e-book enhanced with animations, audio and interactive exercises, Teacher's Manuals and a Test Generator for to facilitate creation of assessment papers. We hope teachers and learners would find this series purposeful in meeting their learning and curriculum objectives. We value your association with us, and welcome your feedback on the series.

To share your feedback, please e-mail us at schoolmarketing.collins@harpercollins-india.com

CONTENTS

SEMESTER 1

SEMESTER 2

Semester 1

1. Globes and Maps

Textbook Reference: Pages 259–264 | **Time Required: 5 periods**

Concepts

Types of maps, globe, axis, symbols, key

Teaching Materials

Posters on maps, worksheets, model of globe, charts and pictures

Learning outcomes

After this lesson, students will be able to:

- Understand the difference between a map and a globe
- Understand the types of maps
- Learn to locate places
- Learn to draw map of their school

Periods	Methodology	Assess
Period 1 **Concepts:** Globes, map, axle	Hang a map and place a globe on the table and tell students that they will learn about them in today's class. Ask students to answer the questions in **Take off** and **Warm up.** Globe is mounted on an axle so that it can spin just like the Earth spins on its axis. A map is a drawing of the Earth's surface or a part of it on a flat surface. Maps are useful when we want to study only a part of the Earth or a specific country.	• Define a map and globe • Explain the uses of map and globe. • Locate the Arabian Sea, the Bay of Bengal and the Indian Ocean on a map.
Period 2 **Concept:** Types of maps	Maps are primarily of three kinds. Physical maps show natural features of the Earth, such as mountains, plateaus, plains, rivers and oceans.	• Make a chart showing map symbols.

	Political maps show cities, towns and villages, and different countries and states with their boundaries. Thematic maps provide specific information of rainfall, vegetation, industries and minerals.	
Period 3 **Concept:** Symbols, scale, directions	Some of the components of a map are scale, directions, signs, symbols and colours The teacher explains about the symbols, key, cardinal directions and sub-directions. Why colours are used in a map? Discuss colours used in a map. The teacher recalls the types of map and makes students to differentiate the map and globe.	• Define the term scale. • Students are asked to make compass showing all directions.
Period 4	Ask students to complete the activities and answer the questions in **Do It Yourself**, **Find out**, **Think** and **Enjoy**.	
Period 5	Ask the students to answer the questions in **Work out**.	

2. Latitudes and Longitudes

Textbook Reference: Pages 265–270 | **Time Required: 6 periods**

Concepts

Parallels of latitude, lines of longitude, imaginary lines, hemisphere, prime meridian

Teaching Materials

Map, globe, whiteboard, worksheets

Learning Outcomes

After this lesson, students will be able to:

- Define latitudes and longitudes
- Mark the important lines of latitude
- Define prime meridian

Periods	Methodology	Assess
Period 1 and 2 **Concepts:** Parallels of latitude, lines of longitude, equator, hemisphere	Begin the class by pointing out the imaginary lines on a globe. Ask students to answer the questions in **Take off** and **Warm up.** The imaginary lines running horizontal from east to west are called the lines of latitude. The lines running vertically from the north to the south are called the lines of longitude. The distance between the lines of latitude is always the same. They are also called parallels of latitudes. The 0° latitude is called the equator. It is the longest latitude. The equator divides the Earth into two equal parts. The part of the Earth between the North Pole and the equator is called the Northern Hemisphere. The part of the Earth between the South Pole and the equator is called the Southern Hemisphere.	• Define the parallels of latitude and lines of longitude. • Which latitude divides the earth into two equal parts?

Period 3 **Concepts:** Meridians, Greenwich Meridian	There are four other important parallels of latitudes. Tropic of Cancer (23½°N) Tropic of Capricorn (23½°S) Arctic Circle (66½° N) **Antarctic Circle** (66½° S) The lines of longitude meet at a point at the north and south poles. They are also called meridians. The 0° **longitude** is the prime meridian or Greenwich meridian the teacher shows the same in the map.	• Name the four important parallels of latitude. • Locate the lines of latitude in the given map. • Draw a globe and mark the latitudes on it.
Period 4 **Concepts:** Locating places	How to locate a place? The point where the latitude and the longitude of a place **intersect** each other is the exact location of that place. **Activity** The students are asked to locate their state and India in a given atlas. The teacher recalls what was taught by questioning the students.	
Period 5	Ask students to complete the activities and answer the questions in **Do It Yourself**, **Find out**, **Think** and **Enjoy**.	
Period 6	Ask the students to answer the questions in **Work out**.	

3. Movements of the Earth

Textbook Reference: Pages 271–276 **Time Required: 6 periods**

Concepts

Rotation, revolution, orbit, axis

Teaching Materials

Globe, pictures, map

Learning Outcomes

After this lesson, students will be able to:

- Learn the effects of rotation and revolution
- Learn the movement of the Earth on its axis
- Learn the movements of the Earth
- Learn how the ocean currents are caused

Periods	Methodology	Assess
Period 1 **Concept:** Rotation	Begin the class by asking questions: • How is the day and night caused? • How are the seasons caused? **Demonstration** Teacher does a demonstration with the candle and a globe in the center, the side facing the candle gets the light hence it is day and the other side becomes dark and it is night. Ask students to answer the questions in **Take off** and **Warm up.**	• How are days and nights caused? • Define rotation.
Period 2 **Concept:** Revolution, axis, orbit	Explain with the help of a picture: The Earth moves around the Sun in a fixed path called orbit. This movement is called revolution. How does the Earth spin?	• What is an axis? • How are seasons caused?

	Earth also spins like a top on its own axis. The axis is the imaginary line passing through the centre of the Earth joining the North Pole and the South Pole. This spinning movement of the Earth is called rotation. How is seasons caused?	
Period 3 and 4 **Concept:** Solstice, equinox, winter solstice	We know that the revolution of the Earth causes seasons. Every year the Earth has special positions known as solstices and equinoxes. Explain the solstice and equinox. On 21 June every year, the Northern Hemisphere tilts towards the Sun. All regions in the Southern Hemisphere experience winter during this time. This position of the Earth is called the summer solstice. On 22 December every year, the Tropic of Capricorn receives the direct rays of the Sun as the South Pole tilts towards it. The reverse condition occurs in the Northern Hemisphere, which experiences winter at this time. This position of the Earth is called the winter solstice. The direct rays of the Sun fall on the equator twice a year, on 21 March and 23 September. At this position, neither of the Poles are tilted towards the Sun. As a result, the entire Earth experiences equal days and equal nights. This condition is called an equinox. Recall the lesson with the help of a flowchart.	• What are solstices and equinoxes? • Students are asked to draw the sun and Earth and show the day and night effect.
Period 5	Ask students to complete the activities and answer the questions in **Do It Yourself**, **Find out**, **Think** and **Enjoy**.	
Period 6	Ask the students to answer the questions in **Work out**.	

LESSON PLAN

4. Continents and Oceans

Textbook Reference: Pages 277–284 **Time Required: 7 periods**

Concepts

Continents, oceans, Pangea, Eurasia, Australasia

Teaching Materials

Map, atlas, pictures

Learning Outcomes

After this lesson, students will be able to:

- Understand the location of continents
- Know about the ocean life
- Know the use of land and learn to protect it

Periods	Methodology	Assess
Period 1 **Concepts:** Huge landmasses, continents, Pangea	Start the class with a continent song. Show a world map and then explain the following: Millions of years ago, there was only one huge continent called Pangea, which later split to form the seven continents that we know today. Ask students to answer the questions in **Take off** and **Warm up.**	• Define the term continent.
Period 2 and 3 **Concepts:** Continents, oceans	How many continents and oceans are there in the world? There are seven continents on the Earth—Asia, Europe, Africa, North America, South America, Australia and Antarctica.	• Name the seven continents. • How many oceans are there? Name them.

	The huge water bodies on the Earth's surface are called oceans. There are five oceans on the Earth—the Pacific Ocean, the Atlantic Ocean, the Indian Ocean, the Arctic Ocean and the Antarctic Ocean. The teacher further explains about each continent in detail and shows the map and location. Point out the oceans and explains that the continents Asia and Europe are together referred to as Eurasia. Question: Which continent is called the frozen continent?	
Period 4 and 5 **Concepts:** Eurasia, land and oceans and their importance	The teacher talks about Antarctica and Australia which is called an island continent. The students are asked to speak on the importance of land and ocean. The teacher explains that land is important for people. Landmasses on the Earth's surface are made up of rocks and minerals. While rocks can be used for different types of construction, minerals find a variety of uses in industries and fuels. Land also provides us soil, which is vital for cultivation and is also a place to live. Oceans are important as they are home to a wide variety of marine life, which is a source of livelihood for many people around the world. The teacher conducts a quiz and recalls the main points of the lesson	• Which islands put together are called Australasia? • ______ is called the island continent. • Mark the continents and oceans on a world map. • Make a flashcard on continent with facts.
Period 6	Ask students to complete the activities and answer the questions in **Do It Yourself**, **Find out**, **Think** and **Enjoy**.	
Period 7	Ask the students to answer the questions in **Work out**.	

5. Climatic Zones of the Earth

Textbook Reference: Pages 285–292 **Time Required: 7 periods**

Concepts

Weather, climate, seasons, altitude

Teaching Materials

Pictures, videos, maps, atlas

Learning Outcomes

After this lesson, students will be able to:

- Know the difference between weather and climate
- Understand the climatic zones and their location
- Learn the reasons of climate changes

Concepts	Methodology	Assess
Period 1 **Concept:** Weather	Begin the lesson by asking few questions: • Why do we sweat some days and feel cold some days? • Why some places are cold all through the year? • How are the seasons caused? Ask students to answer the questions in **Take off** and **Warm up.**	Define weather.
Period 2 **Concept:** Climate, altitude	Movement of the Earth around the Sun causes seasons. Explain the reasons for climate change. • The distance from the equator. • Altitude of the place • Distance from the sea. • Direction of wind	• Define climate. • What is altitude? • What is a sea breeze? • What is a land breeze?

Period 3 **Concept:** Climatic zones	She explains about the sea breeze and land breeze. Cool air from the sea rushes in to fill the vacuum over the land. It is called the sea breeze. The warm air above the sea rises up and cooler air from the land rushes in to take its place. This is called land breeze. The map is hung and the various climate zones are shown and the latitudes are marked.	• Name the the main climatic zones. • Students are asked to make a model depicting the zones as a group activity.
Period 4 and 5 **Concepts:** Hemispheres	**Torrid Zone** The northern part between 0° and 23½°N is called the North Torrid Zone, and the southern part between 0° and 23½°S is called the South Torrid Zone. **Temperate Zone** The Temperate Zone extends from the Tropic of Cancer to the Arctic Circle (66½°N) in the Northern Hemisphere and from the Tropic of Capricorn to the Antarctic Circle (66½°S) in the Southern Hemisphere **Frigid Zone** The Frigid Zone lies between the Arctic Circle and the North Pole (90°N) in the Northern Hemisphere, and between the Antarctic Circle and the South Pole (90°S) in the Southern Hemisphere. The climate and the countries located in these zones are discussed with students. **Activity** Ask students to mark the countries and zones in the map after referring to the atlas.	
Period 6	Ask students to complete the activities and answer the questions in **Do It Yourself**, **Find out**, **Think** and **Enjoy**.	
Period 7	Ask the students to answer the questions in **Work out**.	

6. The Equatorial Region

Textbook Reference: Pages 293–297 **Time Required: 7 periods**

Concepts

Equatorial region, vegetation, climate, wildlife, rainforest

Teaching Materials

Pictures, atlas, videos

Learning Outcomes

After this lesson, students will be able to:

- Know the location of the region
- Understand the climate condition of the region
- Learn about the vegetation and wildlife in the region

Periods	Methodology	Assess
Period 1 **Concept:** Equatorial region	Teacher shows the map and marks the countries falling in the region. She shows the location of the region in the map. The equatorial region is located between the equator and the Tropic of Cancer (23½°N) in the Northern Hemisphere and between the equator and the Tropic of Capricorn (23½°S) in the Southern Hemisphere. Ask students to answer the questions in **Take off** and **Warm up.**	• Where is the equatorial region located?
Period 2 **Concept:** Climate	The equatorial region experiences a tropical climate with high temperature and humidity. The climate is hot and wet throughout the year as the region receives direct rays of the Sun.	• What is the climate of the region?

Period 3 and 4 **Concepts:** Evergreen forest, rainforest	The equatorial region has some of the densest forests in the world. Not all trees shed leaves at the same time, so these thick rainforests always remain green and hence, are also known as evergreen forests. Explain the different layers: emergent layer, canopy, understorey and forest floor. The equatorial rainforests have a diverse wildlife. Students are asked to name some of the animals.	• Name some of the crops grown in the equatorial region.
Period 5 **Concepts:** The tribes, life in the rain forest, crops and other resources	The rainforests are sparsely populated. The people that live here belong to different tribes that are either hunter-gatherers or farmers. The Pygmies stay in the Congo region, the Semangs in Malaysia and the Yanomano in Brazil. The teacher also adds the crops and minerals grown in this region. **Activity** Map marking is given followed by an assignment. Use a flowchart to recall the lesson.	Make a chart on the resources found in this region.
Period 6	Ask students to complete the activities and answer the questions in **Do It Yourself**, **Find out**, **Think** and **Enjoy**.	
Period 7	Ask the students to answer the questions in **Work out**.	

7. Temperate Grasslands

Textbook Reference: Pages 298–303 **Time Required: 8 periods**

Concepts

Temperate grasslands, climate, vegetation, wildlife, life in grasslands, prairies

Teaching Materials

Pictures, atlas, videos, maps

Learning Outcomes

After this lesson, students will be able to:

- Understand the location of the region
- Understand the type of vegetation and the climate condition
- Know about the wildlife
- Learn about the prairies and the crops grown

Periods	Methodology	Assess
Period 1 **Concept:** Temperate grasslands	Begin the class by explaining that the temperate grasslands are found in both the Southern Hemisphere and the Northern Hemisphere. Name the countries where grasslands are found. In the Northern Hemisphere, they are spread across Asia, Europe and North America. In the Southern Hemisphere, they are found in South America, Australia, New Zealand and South Africa.	• Where are the temperate grasslands located? • Name the countries where the grasslands are found.

Period 2 and 3 **Concept:** Climate, vegetation	This continental type of climate is characterized by hot summers, cold winters and little rainfall. The vegetation in the temperate grasslands primarily includes tall and short grasses. Tall grasses grow in areas that receive heavy rainfall, while short grasses grow in areas that have a continental climate.	• What is the type of climate found in this region?
Period 4 and 5 **Concept:** Wildlife, life in the equatorial region	Ask the the students about the animals found in this region. Since the grasslands have rich soil, people here grow a variety of food crops such as corn, wheat, barley, oats and soybean. People in the grasslands live on huge farms that are called ranches.	• Name some animals found in this region. • Name the crops grown in this equatorial region. • What is a ranch?
Period 6 **Concept:** Prairies	Teacher discusses about the prairies. The vast grasslands in North America, also known as prairies, extend from Canada to Mexico Prairies are also called the wheat basket of the world as the surplus is exported to other nations. Used mainly as grazing grounds, the prairies are now one of the largest cultivated lands in the world and have mechanized farms. Corn, wheat, barley, oats, rye are some of the important crops grown here. Cattle rearing are another important occupation in this region. Assignment is given to the students	• Which river flows in the prairie? • Name the crops cultivated in the prairie. • Mark in the map the countries having temperate grasslands.
Period 7	Ask students to complete the activities and answer the questions in **Do It Yourself**, **Find out**, **Think** and **Enjoy**.	
Period 8	Ask the students to answer the questions in **Work out**.	

8. Desert Region

Textbook Reference: Pages 304–308 **Time Required: 6 periods**

Concepts

Desert, hot desert, cold desert, climate, vegetation, wildlife, life of people in the region

Teaching Materials

Map, atlas, pictures

Learning Outcomes

After this lesson, students will be able to

- Understand the difference between the hot and cold desert region
- Know about the conditions which help people and animals to live in the place
- Know the reasons for climate conditions and the vegetation in these regions

Periods	Methodology	Assess
Period 1 **Concept:** Desert region	Begin the class by asking questions: Have you seen a desert? Name it. If so how was the place hot or cold? Explain: A desert is a large area of land that has very little water and very few plants. Ask students to answer the questions in **Take off** and **Warm up.**	• Define a desert.
Period 2, 3 and 4 **Concepts:** Hot desert, climate, vegetation, wildlife, life of people	Ask the students to read the text and find the location of the hot desert and cold desert. **Activity** Students are asked to mark the countries with hot desert in the map.	• Why is there a huge difference between day and night temperatures in hot deserts? • Name the countries with hot deserts. • Name some animals found in the desert.

	Climate The climate generally is hot and dry with sparse rains. Daytime temperatures in hot deserts are very high. Cactus, acacia, thorny bushes and baobab are some plants found in deserts. Apart from the camel, animals like foxes, moles, hyenas, snakes, scorpions, lizards and beetles can be seen in the deserts. Do you know camel is called the ship of desert? The camel, also known as the 'ship of the desert', can stay without food and water for long periods of time. Type of crops cultivated: People there cultivate alfalfa, vegetables, dates, barley and rye. The most popular food crop is millet and it is grown near water holes. Wheat and barley are grown near the oases. **Resources** Petroleum deposits are found in Saudi Arabia, Iran, Iraq and the Sahara Desert. Have a a quiz to recall the key points in the lesson.	• What type of crops are cultivated in this region
Period 5	Ask students to complete the activities and answer the questions in **Do It Yourself**, **Find out**, **Think** and **Enjoy**.	
Period 6	Ask the students to answer the questions in **Work out**.	

9. Frigid Zone

Textbook Reference: Pages 309–314 | **Time Required: 6 periods**

Concepts

Frigid Zone, north and south frigid zone, climate, life in the frigid zone

Teaching Materials

Map, atlas, pictures

Learning Outcomes

- Explain the location and countries in the frigid zone
- Describe the climate condition in the region

Periods	Methodology	Assess
Period 1 **Concepts:** Frigid Zone, north and south frigid zone	On a map, point out the location of frigid zone and explain: The North Frigid Zone is located between the Arctic Circle and the North Pole, that is, between 66 ½°N and 90°N latitudes. The South Frigid Zone is located between the Antarctic Circle and the South Pole, that is, between 66 ½°S and 90°S latitudes. Ask students to answer the questions in **Take off** and **Warm up.**	• Where are the north and south frigid zones located? • Name the countries located in the north and south frigid zones.
Period 2 **Concept:** Climatic condition	Ask the students to check the atlas and find countries located in these regions. The Frigid Zones get less intense sunrays, which are spread over a wide area. These regions are covered with glaciers and a thick layer of ice called the ice cap. The climate here remains very cold throughout the year. During the summer months when the snow melts, a few flower-bearing plants, shrubs bearing berries, mosses, lichens and grasses can be seen.	• What is an ice cap? • Name some animals that live in this region.

Period 3 and 4 **Concept:** Wildlife, life of people, tribes	Animals have a thick coat of fur covering their bodies as it helps them survive the bitter cold. Most of them are nomadic hunters. Fishing is a common practice in these areas. Some of the tribes living in the Frigid Zone include Yakuts, Samoyeds, Chukchis in Siberia, Aleuts in Alaska in the USA, Inuit in Greenland and the Lapps in Northern Scandinavia. Do you know how they travelled in this region? People depended on sledges pulled by reindeers or wolf-like dogs called huskies for transportation. But these days motorized sledges and motorized boats are also used. Would you like to live in such a place? The students give different answers and the class ends with a group discussion and finally. Recall all the main points of the lesson.	• Name the tribes who live in frigid zone. • How did people travel from one place to other? • Mark the countries in the frigid zone. • Make a chart of pictures of animals, people and crops that live and grow in frigid zone.
Period 5	Ask students to complete the activities and answer the questions in **Do It Yourself**, **Find out**, **Think** and **Enjoy**.	
Period 6	Ask the students to answer the questions in **Work out**.	

Values Corner

Textbook Reference: Pages 320–321 **Time Required: 2 periods**

INTEGRITY

Concepts

Integrity, truthful, courage, honest

Teaching Materials

Story chart, pictures, videos

Learning Outcomes

- Learn to define integrity
- Understand the value of honesty and truthful
- Develop courageous attitude

Concepts	Methodology	Assessment
Integrity	Introduce the word integrity with a story chart. Read the story and asks students to identify the values in the story.	Draw a picture or write a poem that represents integrity.
Moral principles	Explain that Integrity is the quality of being honest and firm in moral principles. We should always be truthful. Being honest requires a lot of courage, do not shy away from it.	Make a collage with pictures depicting integrity.
Being honest	Provide groups of students with pages from newspapers. Preview newspapers to make sure they contain at least a few stories that readily raise questions of integrity.	Write words that are synonyms of integrity.

Courage	Point out and discuss key ideas in the story/ video, such as being honest with yourself and with other people. Have students connect this to their understanding of integrity: Why is honesty so important to integrity—knowing and doing what's right? Ask students to explain why they think integrity will be important to their careers. For example, students who aspire to be teachers might recognize that they will serve as role models. Behaving with integrity will help their students learn to do the same. Make them understand that unity and integrity makes the Nation stronger	Complete activity given in the value card.

RESPONSIBILITY

Concepts

Responsibility, duties, self-respect, acceptance

Teaching Materials

Pictures, storybooks, duty list, flashcards

Learning Outcomes

- Learn to define responsibility
- Learn to do the duty
- Accept to job and meet the requirement properly

Concepts	**Methodology**	**Assessment**
Responsibility	*The willingness to accept responsibility of one's own life is a source of self-respect.* The teacher writes the quotation on board and discusses.	Students are asked give a talk for 2 minutes on why we should be responsible.
Trait	Acquaint with the students and tell them which trait you will be discussing today. Ask few questions and call on different students for answers What is responsibility? What are you responsible for?	Students are asked to read a story and share the same with others.

Self-respect	• Own actions • Possessions • Family • Homework • Community • The Nation	Prepare a chart showing the list of responsibilities at home and at school.
Care and commitment	What are ways you can show responsibility? Take care of the things and those of other people. Complete the homework on time without being reminded.	Group work is given to students to complete a chart each one is given a role to complete.
Learn from mistakes	Follow through on your commitments, even when you don't feel like it. Accept responsibility for your mistakes and learn from them. Don't make excuses or blame others.	Create a banner on responsibility with a quotation on it.

DETERMINATION

Concepts

Determination, decision, success, firm

Teaching Materials

Story chart, video clippings of great achievers, pictures

Learning Outcomes

- Learn to be firm in getting things done on right time
- Learn to be determined in all work taken
- Learn to take decisions
- Define the term determination

Concepts	Methodology	Assessment
Determination	Determination is the quality that our show when you have decided to do.	Ask students to write their own story about an animal who uses determination.

Courage	Determination and success go hand in hand. Write the word determination on the board. Ask what is determination?	Ask students to share incidents of determination.
Decision	Include a picture of the successful people at the top of the wall. Spend time explaining what courage and purpose mean using words like, try hard, focus, and not giving up. Offer examples of determination from your own life.	Ask students to make a chart of successful people.
Success	Can you give an example from your life when you were determined? Ask how can determination help us?	Complete the activity given in the value card.
Focus	Show them the determination wall you have created, set up alongside a bookshelf. Explain that all the successful people will be placed at the top of the wall as a reminder of determination.	Make a graphic organizer
Try Hard	Ask what will you think of when you see our wall with all the people on top? When will you use determination? Have a group discussion	In each circle, write what determination means to you. Write a to do list to be determined.

PATRIOTISM

Concepts

Patriotism, loyalty, respect, national spirit

Teaching Materials

Pictures of leaders, chart showing national symbols, maps

Learning Outcomes

- Feeling proud
- Takes pride of being the citizen
- Learns the importance of symbols
- Makes picture of the leaders

Concepts	Methodology	Assessment
Patriotism	*The more we sweat in peace, the less we bleed in war.*	Define patriotism.
Respect the national symbols	The teacher writes the quote on the board and asks students to reflect on it. Further she explains that patriotism is love for your country and loyalty towards it. We should respect the heroes of our country. We should respect all our national symbols.	How would you show your love to the nation?
Love the nation	Think about the different things that you are proud of. You might be proud to be a student at your school. You might be proud to be on a team.	Make a collage showing the leaders of the nation and freedom fighters.
Citizen	You might be proud to be a member of your family. Are you also proud to be a citizen of the Nation?	Complete the activity given in the value card.
Appreciate	If so, this is a display of patriotism. Loving and appreciating your country is a very patriotic attitude.	
Pride	Show the National Flag and other symbols and ask the students to draw and color the national flag. Train the students to stand and recite the pledge in the class. They are taught to appreciate the monuments, work of the military people, national leaders and other contributors of the country. Ask the students to speak about the Independence Day, Republic Day and other National importance events. Make the students to feel pride in the nation and end the class with slogan: 'My Nation My Pride'	

1. GLOBES AND MAPS

A Define the following.

1. Globe
2. Scale
3. Key
4. Map

B Match the following.

Column A	Column B
1. Scale	a. Drawing of earth surface
2. Symbols	b. Features of a place
3. Globe	c. List of symbols
4. Key	d. Calculate distance
5. Map	e. Axle

C Write short notes on the following.

1. Directions
2. Scale
3. Colours
4. Key
5. Physical map

D Draw a globe and mark the four cardinal directions.

Name: .... Teacher's signature: ....

Class: .... Date: ....

2. LATITUDES AND LONGITUDES

A Fill in the blanks.

1. Longitudes are measured in ....
2. All longitudes are .... in length.
3. The .... passes through the Royal Observatory at Greenwich in England.
4. Parallels and meridians crisscross to form a ....
5. The 0° latitude is called the ....

B Write the degrees of each of these latitudes.

1. Tropic of Cancer ....
2. Tropic of Capricorn ....
3. Arctic Circle ....
4. Antarctic Circle ....
5. Equator ....

C Answer these questions.

1. Name the continents through which the equator passes.
2. Name the four important latitudes.
3. State two important facts about latitudes.
4. What is the International Date Line?
5. How can we locate a place on a map?

Name: .... Teacher's signature: ....

Class: .... Date: ....

3. MOVEMENTS OF THE EARTH

A Define the following.

1. Rotation
2. Revolution
3. Axis
4. Orbit

B Fill in the blanks.

1. The Earth rotates on its ....
2. The Earth takes .... to complete one rotation.
3. The Sun is in a fixed path called ....
4. .... is the imaginary line passing through the Earth.
5. This spinning movement of the Earth is called ....

C Match the following.

Column A	Column B
1. Orbit	a. Seasons
2. Axis	b. Planet
3. Rotation	c. Fixed path
4. Revolution	d. Imaginary line
5. Solar system	e. Day and night

D Answer the following.

1. What is summer solstice?
2. What is equinox?

Name: .... Teacher's signature: ....

Class: .... Date: ....

ADDITIONAL WORKSHEET

4. CONTINENTS AND OCEANS

A **Make the oceans and continents of the world on the world map.**

B **Fill in the blanks.**

1. .... is also called the 'island continent'.
2. .... is the largest ocean in the world.
3. The Atlantic Ocean is an .... ocean.
4. .... is the only ocean to be named after a country.
5. .... is the densest rainforest in the world.

C **Answer these questions.**

1. Why is Australia called an Island continent?
2. Why is Antarctica called the 'frozen continent'?
3. Write the significance of African continent.
4. Name some of the oceans that surround South America.
5. Name the rivers that flow into the Indian Ocean.

Name: .... Teacher's signature: ....

Class: .... Date: ....

5. CLIMATIC ZONES OF THE EARTH

A Fill in the blanks.

1. The moving of the Earth around the Sun causes ....
2. The cool air that comes from the sea is called ....
3. .... Zone receives intense sunlight throughout the year.
4. .... Zone lies between the Arctic Circle and the North Pole.
5. The Temperate Zone extends from the .... to the ....

B Answer these questions.

1. What are factors that affect the climate of a place?
2. How is the sea breeze caused?
3. On what basis are the climatic zones divided?
4. Differentiate between weather and climate.
5. Write a short note on the Frigid Zone.

C Mark the climate zones on the world map.

Name: .... Teacher's signature: ....

Class: .... Date: ....

ADDITIONAL WORKSHEET

6. THE EQUATORIAL REGION

A Answer these questions.

1. Mention the several layers of the plants that grow in rainforests.
2. Mention the names of the animals that live in rainforests.
3. Name some of the crops grown in equatorial region.
4. Name the different tribes that live in the equatorial region.
5. What is the type of climate in the equatorial region.

B Draw the layers of the trees in a rainforest.

C Write the meanings of these words.

1. Marmoset ....
2. Sparsely ....
3. Decay ....
4. Pygmies ....
5. Canopy ....

D Look at the atlas and name five countries that are in the equatorial region.

Name: .... Teacher's signature: ....

Class: .... Date: ....

7. TEMPERATE GRASSLANDS

A Fill in the blanks.

1. .... are found in both the Southern Hemisphere and the Northern Hemisphere.
2. .... are commonly found in the grasslands of North America.
3. The major occupation of the people in temperate grasslands is .... and ....
4. People in the grasslands live on huge farms that are called ....
5. The vast grasslands in North America are also known as ....

B Match the following.

Column A	Column B
1. Estancias	a. Saudi Arabia
2. Bison	b. North America
3. Rodent	c. Small water bodies
4. Petroleum	d. South America
5. Oasis	e. Small mammal

C Answer the following questions.

1. Write a short note on the Prairies.
2. Write a paragraph on the vegetation in the grasslands.
3. What is continental type of climate?
5. Why are prairies called the 'wheat basket of the world'.

D On the given, map mark grasslands of the world.

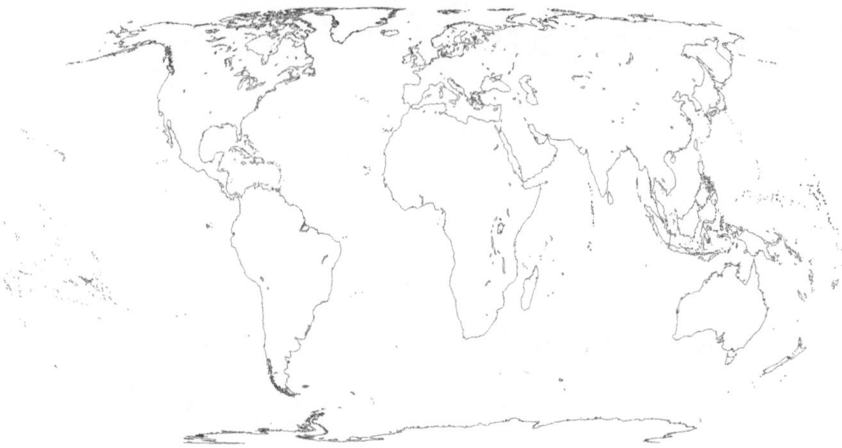

Name: .... Teacher's signature: ....

Class: .... Date: ....

8. DESERT REGION

A **Match the following.**

Column A	Column B
1. Camel	a. Water body
2. Sahara	b. Ship of the desert
3. Gobi	c. Thorny plant
4. Oasis	d. Asia
5. Cactus	e. Africa

B **Write the missing letters.**

1. K A__ A __A RI DESERT
2. SA __ A __A DESERT
3. PA__A G__NI_N DESERT
4. M E__ I C__ DESERT
5. G __ ___ I DESERT

C **Give one-word answers.**

1. A large area of land ....
2. Small water bodies ....
3. Ship of the desert ....
4. Hot desert in Australia ....
5. Cold desert in Asia ....

Name: .... Teacher's signature: ....

Class: .... Date: ....

9. FRIGID ZONE

A Fill in the blanks.

1. The North Frigid Zone is located between .... and ....
2. The South Frigid Zone is located between .... and ....
3. .... is called the frozen continent.
4. The Sun rises and sets only once in a year in the areas around the ....
5. Greenland is located in the ....

B Answer these questions.

1. Name the countries that are located in the North Frigid Zone.
2. Write a note on the climate of the Frigid Zone.
3. Name the tribes that live in the Frigid Zone.
4. Name the plants that grow in the Frigid Zone.
5. Name the animals that live in the Frigid Zone.

C Mark the following countries on the map of the world.

Greenland, Northern Canada, Northern Alaska and Northern Scandinavia, which includes Norway, Sweden, Finland, Iceland and Northern Siberia in Russia.

Name: .... Teacher's signature: ....

Class: .... Date: ....

ADDITIONAL WORKSHEET

Coursebook Answers

1 Globes and Maps

Take off

- The Earth is the third planet in the solar system.
- Like the other planets, it travels around the Sun.

Warm up

This represents the four cardinal directions.

Do it yourself

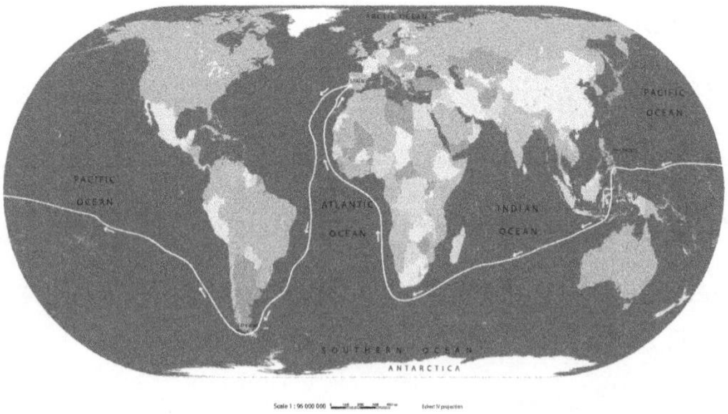

Workout

A 1. a 2. a 3. b 4. a

B 1. globe 2. political maps
3. thematic maps
4. north 5. legend

C 1. T 2. F 3. F 4. F 5. F

D
1. The four components of a map are scale, directions, signs and symbols, and colours.
2. The term cardinal directions means the main directions which are north, south, west and east.
3. The sub-directions are north-west, north-east, south-west and south-east.
4. All the maps have signs and symbols that are used all over the world. These symbols are very important because they provide a lot of information in very little space. One can read the maps easily by using these symbols.
5. There are three different kinds of maps – physical maps, political maps and thematic maps. The physical maps show the different natural features of Earth like mountains, plateaus, river, oceans, etc. Cities, towns, villages, countries and states are shown in the political maps. Thematic maps provide specific information such as road maps, rainfall and distribution of natural vegetation, industries, minerals and others.
6. All maps around the world have a definite colour scheme that is accepted all around the world. They show different landforms and heights in maps. Water bodies are normally shown in blue and the colour brown is used to show regions where there are mountains and hills.

Think

1. Google Maps
2. It shows us where we are and how we can reach our next destination.
3. A smartphone with GPS

Enjoy

Down: 1. scale 2. globe
3. physical 4. thematic

Across: 3. political 5. legend 6. map

Life Skills and Values

Students will do on their own

2 Latitudes and Longitudes

Take off

- Large landmasses on the Earth are called landforms.
- About 70 per cent of the Earth's surface is covered by water.

* These are suggested answers hence accept other valid answers too.

Warm up

It is a physical map.

Find out

The Equator passes through South America, Asia and Africa. The Equator does not pass through North America, Australia, Europe and Antarctica.

Do it yourself

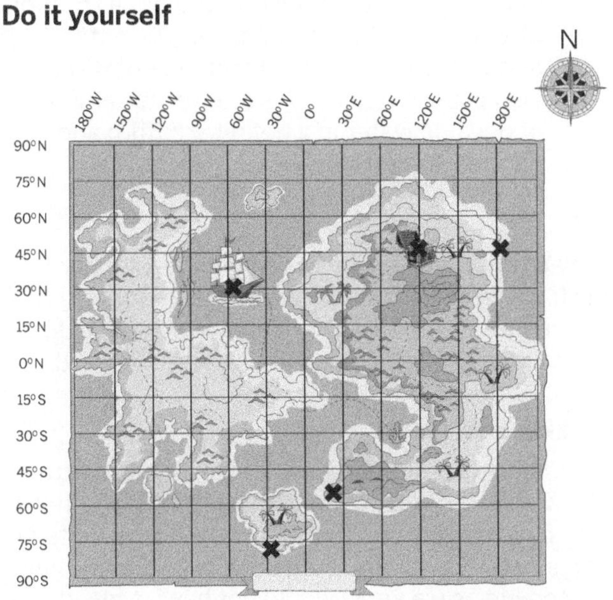

Workout

A 1. a 2. a 3. a 4. b 5. a

B 1. Prime Meridian 2. North pole 3. Northern hemisphere 4. Tropic of Cancer 5. grid

C 1. F 2. F 3. T 4. F 5. T

D

1. Equator is the parallel of latitude that runs midway through the Earth. It is the 0° latitude and divides the Earth into two equal halves or hemispheres.
2. Parallels of latitude are the circles of latitude which run parallel to each other.

   The latitudes are also known as parallels of latitude since the distance between two latitudes mostly stays the same other than at the poles where they are just dots.
3. A meridian is the half of an imaginary circle on the Earth's surface, terminated by the North Pole and the South Pole, connecting points of equal longitude, as measured in angular degrees east or west of the Prime Meridian.
4. We can find the location of a place with latitude and longitude by seeing where these two intersect each other.
5. The International Date Line is an imaginary line of demarcation on the surface of Earth that runs from the North Pole to the South Pole and demarcates the change of one calendar day to the next.
6. The two hemispheres of the Earth are the Northern Hemisphere and the Southern Hemisphere.

Think

No, all countries in the world do not follow the same time. Time is normally determined on the basis of days and nights and every country does not have day and night at the same time. This is why if all countries in the world followed the same time it would mean that a country would have to accept day as night.*

Life skills and values

1. The climate at the Arctic is always extremely cold, with the winter months being just unbearable. It is important to wear at least four layers of clothing, have the ability to detect diseases such as frostbite and frost nip. You should be able to put off animals such as polar bears. You should also have sufficient fuel and you should be able to understand the condition of the ice. You should not travel in big groups and should have equipment like GPS, alert bacons, and satellite phones. Sleeping bags and dry suits are important as well.*
2. Our country India has mostly warm climate but there are certain locations where the climate is fairly cold. This is how our country is different from the Arctic Circle.*
3. I think it would be possible to communicate with my friends and family using letters, emails, phone calls, etc.*

3 Movements of the Earth

Take off

- The imaginary line passing through the centre of the Earth is called the equator.
- The prime meridian passes through Greenwich in England

Warm up

North Pole and South Pole

Find out

Countries like Alaska in extreme north and those in extreme south enjoy 24 hours daylight in summer. This country is located in the continent of North America.

Workout

A 1. b. 2. a. 3. a. 4. a. 5. a.

B
1. revolution
2. axis
3. Southern Hemisphere
4. orbit
5. leap year

C 1. F 2. F 3. T 4. T 5. F

D
1. Rotation is the movement of the Earth on its own axis.
2. An axis is the imaginary line on which the Earth rotates.
3. The summer solstice occurs on 21 June.
4. The days and nights are of equal length during autumn and spring equinoxes when Sun rays are equal.
5. Southern Hemisphere experiences summer when the Northern Hemisphere experiences winter.
6. Effects of Earth's revolution include the seasons and variation in the length of days and nights.
7. Summer solstice takes place on 21 June. On this day the Northern Hemisphere tilts towards the Sun and its rays fall straight on the Tropic of Cancer. This is why areas that are located on this latitude get more heat and have the summer season. Since the North Pole is tilted towards the Sun, places that are located in the Arctic Circle get continued daylight for six months straight. At this time the Southern Hemisphere has winter.
   Winter solstice takes place on 22 December. On this day direct sunrays fall on the Tropic of Capricorn since the South Pole is tilting toward the Sun. This means that a lot of Southern Hemisphere receives sunlight on this day. At this time the hemisphere has shorter nights and longer days since it is the summer season over there. During this time the Northern Hemisphere has winter.
8. Rotation is the movement of Earth on its axis, which is tilted at an angle of 23 ½°.
   Earth spins from west to east and this is why we are able to see the Sun rise in the east and set in the west. It takes almost 24 hours for Earth to complete one rotation.
   Days and nights are caused by rotation. Since Earth is rotating on its axis, only one half of the same gets sunlight at a time. This is why when some countries have day others have night. Apart from day and night rotation also leads to the flow of ocean currents and winds in a certain direction. Rotation also causes tides. Tides are the rise and fall of oceanic water in a definite rhythm and happen twice a day.

Think

The places in the east see the Sun first since Earth spins from west to east and thus it seems as if the Sun rises in the east. The countries in the east receive sunlight before those in the western part.

Life skills and values

It would be really difficult for life forms to thrive in such conditions. Ideally, life needs proper conditions like heat, cold, rain, etc. to thrive but if some parts of Earth are always hot and some are always extremely cold then life as we know would not have evolved. It could have been a different breed of animals and plants that would have adapted to the conditions and developed likewise.

4 Continents and Oceans

Take off

- There is life on the Earth because it has air and water.
- Earth is called the blue planet.

Warm up

Land and water

Do it yourself

Canada – North America
Ghana – Africa
Peru – South America
England – Europe
Sydney – Asia

Find out

Atlantic and Pacific Oceans

Workout

A 1. b. 2. b. 3. c. 4. b

B 1. Atlantic Ocean 2. Sahara
3. Bering Strait 4. Australia
5. Amazon

C 1. T 2. F 3. F 4. T

D
1. The Equator, Tropic of Cancer, Tropic of Capricorn and Prime Meridian pass through Africa.
2. The term Eurasia refers to the continents of Europe and Asia together. The word Australasia means the continents of Asia and Australia together.
3. Land is important because it has rocks and minerals that are used for various purposes.
4. The Southern Ocean is created after the Pacific, Indian and Atlantic oceans merge together around Antarctica.
5. Asia is the most densely packed continent in the world. Asia has both India and China which are two of the most populated nations in the world. Also, Asia is the largest continent, hence, a large number of the world's population resides here.
6. The Atlantic Ocean has an irregular coastline. This is why it is convenient for building harbours and ports. As a result, it provides excellent locations for ports and harbours. Therefore, its ports have the highest passenger and cargo traffic in the world.
7. Asia is the biggest continent of the world. It is located between 25°E and 170°W longitudes and 80°N and 10°S latitudes. It is surrounded by Pacific Ocean in the east, Indian Ocean in the south and Arctic Ocean in the north. It also accounts for one-third of the entire landmass in the world. The Ural Mountains separate it from Europe. Asia and Europe together are also known as Eurasia. Asia is also the most populated continent in the world – almost 60% of the global population lives here. The range of mountains known as Himalaya is located over here. It is home to Mt Everest, which is one of the tallest peaks in the world.
8. Oceans are home to an unmatched array of marine life such as various kinds of fishes, plants, dolphins, whales, octopuses, squids, sharks and plants. These provide many people around the world their income. They also make sure that the coastal areas have a moderate climate. With the large ships they also serve as media of transportation for cargo and passengers.

Think

1. Penguin
2. They can be found in Antarctica.

Life skills and values

There are two major ways in which oceans get polluted by ships. Firstly they drop garbage in these waters and pollute them. This garbage often has harmful chemicals and other pollutants that cause harm to the marine life forms. Secondly, ships that carry oil often spill that oil and this is even more dangerous. This oil forms a layer that does not allow sunlight to get through and deprives plants underneath the sea the oxygen needed for making food. When these plants are unable to survive, it affects fishes that feed on these and that effects other marine life forms that feed on these fishes.*

5 Climatic Zones of the Earth

Take off

- Rotation causes day and night.
- Revolution causes the change of seasons.

Warm up

Rain

Find out

Arctic fox, polar bear and penguins are some animals found in Frigid Zone.

Do it yourself

Continent	Torrid zone	Temperate zone	Frigid zone
Asia	Indonesia	parts of China/ Japan	
Europe		England	Norway
Africa	Ghana		

Workout

A 1. a. 2. a. 3. a. 4. b.

B 1. Antarctica 2. Torrid 3. Frigid
4. Sea breeze 5. Land breeze

C 1. T 2. T 3. F 4. F

ANSWER KEYS

D

1. With greater height, temperatures tend to decrease and the climate becomes cooler.
2. The Torrid Zone is always experiencing high temperatures throughout the year with very little seasonal variation.
3. When a place is very humid it tends to increase the temperatures and the place tends to be very hot.
4. In the Northern Hemisphere Frigid Zone is located between North Pole and Arctic Circle and in the Southern Hemisphere it is located between the South Pole and Antarctic Circle. The first one is known as North Frigid Zone and the second one is referred to as South Frigid Zone. These zones get slanted rays of the Sun, which means lesser intensity of sunlight. This is why these areas have rather cold climate.
5. Coastal areas have moderate climate because of the action of land breeze and sea breeze. In India, places such as Delhi – which are located at some distance from the sea – have an extreme climate, while the climate in Goa and Mumbai – places that are located right next to the sea – have moderate climate. This happens because the seas and oceans absorb the heat of Sun.

   The sea normally takes more time to get heated and become cooler. During the day time the land gets hotter at a faster rate than the sea. As such, the air becomes hot and rises up thus creating a vacuum. The cool breeze from sea rushes in to fill this vacuum. This is called the sea breeze. It blows like an onshore gentle wind. During the night the exact opposite happens. The land cools down quicker than the sea. Thus, the warm air from sea rises up and cool air from land rushes in to fill up the space thus created. This is called the land breeze.
6. There are two temperate zones – North Temperate Zone and South Temperate Zone. The North Temperate Zone is located between Tropic of Cancer and Arctic Circle and the South Temperate Zone is located between Tropic of Capricorn and Antarctic Circle. Compared to the Torrid Zone the Temperate Zone is cooler and drier. There is a lot of difference between temperatures in summer and winter in these areas. This area also receives fairly differing amounts of sunlight at different seasons of the year. The summers have long days and short nights and it is just the opposite during winters.

Think

1. Polar bear
2. It will survive only in extremely cold climate.

Life skills and values

If I had to choose a certain climatic zone I would choose the temperate zone since the climate here is good. It is neither too hot nor too cold and the rainfall is also sufficient.*

Enjoy

Across: 3. curvature 6. altitude 8. climate 9. sea breeze

Down: 1. humidity 2. Frigid 4. land breeze 5. seasons 7. temperate

6 The Equatorial Region

Take off

- There are three major climatic zones in the world.
- India is located in the temperate zone.

Warm up

It is a gorilla. It can be found in the Democratic Republic of the Congo.

Do it yourself

Ecuador, Colombia, Brazil, Gabon, Democratic Republic of the Congo

Find out

People in the rainforests use cassava to make bread which they eat with fish, meat and other food items.*

Workout

A 1. a. 2. a. 3. a. 4. a.

B

1. emergent
2. Brazil
3. Semangs
4. forest floor

C 1. F 2. T 3. T 4. F

D

1. The equatorial region is located between the equator and the Tropic of Cancer (23½°N) in the Northern Hemisphere and between the equator and the Tropic of Capricorn (23½°S) in the Southern Hemisphere. Located in the Torrid Zone, the region receives direct rays of the Sun throughout the year. Tropical

rainforests are located near the equator hence they are also called equatorial rainforests. 57% of all tropical rainforests are found in Latin America. Other tropical rainforests are found in Southeast Asia and the Pacific Islands and West Africa.

2. Gorillas, chimpanzees, monkeys, lemurs, marmosets, flying squirrels, bats and baboons, reptiles such as crocodiles, alligators, snakes and lizards, and hippopotamus and jaguars, birds, giraffes, antelopes and butterflies are found in the Equatorial rainforests.
3. Pygmies, Yanomano and Semangs are some of the various tribes that live in the Equatorial rainforests.
4. The equatorial areas have high humidity and high temperatures around the world.
5. Not too many people live in the rainforests. Most of them belong to different tribes – Pygmies of Congo, Yanomano of Brazil and Semangs of Malaysia. Rice, maize, and cassava are the major crops that they grow. Cash crops such as cocoa, coffee, tobacco, cotton, rubber, and oil palm are grown as well. These areas have plenty of mineral resources as well.
6. Since the equatorial regions are pretty hot and humid one can find different kinds of trees and plants over here. These forests are also known as evergreen forests since not every tree sheds leaves at the same time as the other. These are basically dense forests and over here vegetation grows in different layers. The emergent trees are the tallest and form the uppermost layer. The crowns of these trees form a thick canopy, which is the second layer.
   The third layer is formed by climbers and creepers that can make it hard for one to walk on the floors of these forests. In this area the remains of animals and plants are decomposed by fungi and bacteria thus making the soil rich for plants and helping them survive.

Think

1. Macaw
2. They are found in countries such as Ecuador, Brazil and Colombia.

Life skills and values

Yes, they are extremely important because without them the soil would not be as rich in nutrients and the small climbers and creepers will not get the food that they need to sustain themselves.*

Enjoy

Country selected: Brazil

1. Brazil is officially known as the Federative Republic of Brazil. It is the biggest country in South America and the fifth biggest in the world, in terms of area and population. It is the biggest Portuguese speaking nation and the only one to do so in both North and South America.*
2. Brazil has the typical rainforest – the Amazon rainforest. It also has other major forest systems such as Cerrado – a tropical savanna – and Atlantic Forest, which is a tropical forest as well.*
3. Brazil is surrounded by the Atlantic Ocean in the east. It also shares boundaries with every country in South America other than Chile and Ecuador.*
4. North of Brazil has an Equatorial climate while in the central part one sees a savanna kind of climate and in northeastern parts it is almost semi-arid. In the southern part of Brazil it is pretty cool climate with cold winters and mild summers. At times, these places also see snowfall and frost as well.*
5. Brazil has a diverse vegetation with the northern part having an equatorial vegetation and tropical grasslands in the remaining parts.*
6. Brazil's economy is not as well developed and there is a fair degree of crime rate as well.*
7. The capital of Brazil is Brasilia but its largest city is Sao Paulo. Its President is Dilma Rousseff and the national parliament has two houses. Brazil declared its independence on 7 September 1822 and it was officially recognized on 29 August 1825. It became a republic on 15 November 1889 and its present constitution came into effect on 5 October 1988. It occupies a total area of 8,515,767 km^2.*

7 Temperate Grasslands

Take off

- The Torrid zone experiences a <u>cold</u> climate.
- The Temperate Zone enjoys a <u>moderate</u> climate

Warm up

Australia and New Zealand*

Do it yourself

North America – prairies

South America – pampas
South Africa – veld
Eurasia – steppes
Australia – downs

Find out

Dry conditions and lesser amount of rainfall is the reason for lack of trees in prairies.

Workout

A 1. a. 2. a. 3. a. 4. a.

B 1. cattle 2. estancias 3. veld 4. Mississippi

C 1. T 2. T 3. F 4. F 5. T

D
1. The temperate grasslands receive little rainfall. The summers here are hot and winters are equally cold.
2. The vegetation in the temperate grasslands is inclusive of short and tall grasses.
3. Apart from grazing animals and rodents, bisons, lions, elephants, antelopes, koala bears, kangaroos, wallabies can be found in the temperate grasslands.
4. The temperate grasslands can be seen in both Northern and Southern hemispheres. In the Northern Hemisphere, these grasslands can be seen in Asia, Europe and North America. In the Southern Hemisphere they can be seen in South America, Australia, New Zealand and South Africa.
5. For people who live in the temperate grasslands the main occupations are agriculture and livestock farming. The grasslands are very rich and this is why people grow various food crops like corn, wheat, barley, oats and soyabean. People rear animals in large farms that are known as estancias in South America and homesteads or ranches in Australia and North America. Cattle are reared for meat and dairy products. In Australia sheep rearing is practised for wool and meat.
6. Some of the plants grown in the prairies include corn, wheat, barley, rye, oats, and healthy grass.

Think

1. Two-horned rhinoceros
2. It is not an extinct species. However, it is endangered and very few are found in the wild nowadays. Most of them are found in national sanctuaries and parks where they are protected.

Life skills and values

National parks have been created where bisons can inhabit, some bison hunting is allowed but under controlled conditions, fees have been set up for bison hunting and a permit is required.

Enjoy

Across: 1. Mississippi 6. estancias
Down: 2. Steppes 3. Prairies 4. Ranch 5. Bison

8 Desert Region

Take off

- In desert areas, cactus plants grow. They need very little water to survive.
- Camel is an animal commonly found in deserts.

Warm up

Desert; the region experiences very hot during daytime and cold during nights

Find out

In hot deserts the day temperatures are very hot as the Sun's rays are intense. However, as deserts have no trees and lack of clouds, the land loses its heat very quickly and therefore nights become very cold.

Do it yourself

Students will do themselves

Workout

A 1. a. 2. b. 3. a. 4. b.

B 1. Saudi Arabia 2. Atacama 3. camel 4. millet

C 1. F 2. F 3. T 4. F

D
1. A desert is a barren area of landscape where little precipitation occurs and, consequently, living conditions are hostile for plant and animal life.
2. Camels, snakes, scorpions and lizards are some animals that are found in the desert areas.
3. The plants in desert areas have deep roots, thick stems, and waxy leaves and thorns.
4. Gobi desert, Thar Desert
5. Deserts are characterized by extreme climatic conditions. The climate generally is hot and dry with sparse rains. Daytime temperatures in hot deserts are very high,

particularly in the summer season. Desert regions are also prone to sandstorms.

6. Life in the desert is difficult due to the scarcity of water and extreme climatic conditions. People normally live in or near the oases and move from one oasis to another. Animal herding is the main occupation of these nomadic tribes. People there cultivate alfalfa, vegetables, dates, barley and rye. The most popular food crop is millet and it is grown near water holes. Wheat and barley are grown near the oases. Some deserts are rich in mineral deposits like petroleum and copper. Mining is an important occupation in such regions.

Think

Some plants have green stems in order to aid them with photosynthesis and getting energy from Sun. The green stems produce the plant's food and lose less water than leaves do.

Life skills and values

Limited water in the deserts forces the animals and plants to adapt and survive.*

Enjoy

Students will answer on their own.

Worksheet (Chapters 1–8)

A 1. sailed around; 2. horizontal; 3. rotation; 4. warmer;
5. cartography; 6. evergreen forests.

B 1. c; 2. a; 3. b; 4. e; 5. d

C 1. axle; 2. leap year; 3. intersect; 4. Australasia; 5. land breeze; 6. temperature; 7. Pacific ocean; 8. animal herding; 9. prairies; 10. camel

D 1. understory; 2. Meridians of longitude; 3. 22 December; 4. hot and wet; 5. Temperature Zones

9 Frigid Zone

Take off

- The Frigid zone is the coldest heat zone of the Earth.
- The areas in the Frigid zone remain covered by ice/snow most of the time.

Warm up

Reindeer; Frigid Zone

Do it yourself*

Skiing – ski equipment
Snowboarding – snow board
Skating – skating boots
Sledding – sleds, toboggan
Building a snowman – all you need in snow

Find out

In places where there is no sunlight for six months, the days are like night.

Workout

A	1. b	2. c.	3. b	4. c.
B	1. migrate	2. lichens	3. Inuit	4. husky
C	1. T	2. T	3. T	4. F

D

1. The North Frigid Zone is located between Arctic Circle and North Pole. The South Frigid Zone is located between Antarctic Circle and South Pole.
2. Greenland, Norway, Sweden, Finland and Iceland are countries that are located in the Frigid Zone.
3. Flower-bearing plants, berrie-bearing shrubs, mosses, lichens, dwarf willow and grasses are the vegetation that can be found in the Frigid Zone. Wolves, foxes, voles, squirrels, snowshoe hare, musk ox, ermine and reindeer are the main animals found over here.
4. The Frigid Zones have continued daylight during the summers and continued darkness during the winter.
5. Vegetation in the Frigid Zones is sparse owing to the extreme cold. The vegetation of this area can be classified as tundra. The soil normally remains frozen over here across the year. At the summer time the snow melts and flower-bearing plants, berrie-bearing shrubs, mosses, lichens and grasses can be seen at that time. The only tree that grows here is the dwarf willow. It serves as food for animals.
6. Since the frigid zones are very cold life is extremely difficult for people. Fishing is a common practice. Yakuts, Samoyeds, Chukchis of Siberia, Aleuts of Alaska, Inuits of Greenland and Lapps of Scandinavia are the main tribes living here. Earlier people

used sledges driven by reindeer or huskies, which are wolf like dogs, for transportation. However, motor boats and sledges are used these days.

Think

1. Polar bear
2. Arctic regions

Life skills and values

They use artificial light as we all do during night time.*

Review Corner

A 1. thematic maps; 2. latitudes; 3. 24 hours; 4. Pangea; 5. Curvature of our planet; 6. Amazon; 7. Antarctica; 8. Axle; 9. Dogs that pull sledges; 10. Acacia

B 1. True; 2. False; 3. False; 4. False; 5. True

C
1. Antarctica because it is not a desert.
2. Inuit because they are not a nomadic tribe.
3. Eurasia because it is not an ocean.
4. Prime meridian as it is not a polar circle.
5. Equatorial because it is not a heat zone .

D 1. prairies; 2. oasis; 3. key; 4. equator; 5. Suez Canal

E
1. Oceans produce over half of the world's oxygen and absorbs 50 times more carbon dioxide than our atmosphere. They are also home to a large variety of flora, fauna and aquatic animals.
2. Grasses dominate temperate grasslands. Trees and large shrubs are rarely found in grassland areas. There are many species of grasses that live in this biome, including, purple needle grass, wild oats, foxtail, ryegrass, and buffalo grass.
3. Apart from the camel, animals like foxes, moles, hyenas, snakes, scorpions, lizards and beetles can be seen in the deserts.
4. Earth's rotation is the cause for the differences in daytime and nighttime as it spins on its axis.
5. The days are longer around the summer solstice and shorter around the winter solstice. A solstice is an event occurring when the Sun appears to reach its most northerly or southerly excursion relative to the celestial equator on the celestial sphere. Two solstices occur annually, around June 21 and December 21. An equinox is commonly regarded as the instant of time when the plane of Earth's equator passes through the center of the Sun. This occurs twice each year: around 20 March and 23 September. In other words, it is the moment at which the center of the visible Sun is directly above the equator.

Worksheet Answers

1 Globes and Maps

A
1. It is the model of earth and is mounted on an axle.
2. It is the ratio between the actual distance and ground distance on a map.
3. It is the list of symbols.
4. It is a drawing of the Earth's surface or a part of it on a flat surface.

B
1. d 2. b 3. e
4. c 5. a

C
1. Directions are important in a map. There are four cardinal directions and four sub directions. They help us to locate place accurately.
2. A scale is the ratio between the actual distance on the ground and the distance shown on the map, it helps us calculate the distance between any two places on a map.
3. All maps use a standard colour scheme to depict various landforms and altitudes in map.
4. It is also called as legend, they are symbols used within the map and what they stand for.
5. They show natural features of the earth such as mountains, plateaus, plains, rivers and oceans.

2 Latitudes and Longitudes

A
1. Degrees 2. Equal 3. Prime meridian
4. Grid 5. Equator

B
1. 23½ ° N 2. 23½ °S 3. 66 ½ °N
4. 66 ½ ° S 5. 0 °

C
1. The equator passes through the continents of South America, Africa and Asia.
2. Tropic of cancer
   Tropic of Capricorn
   Arctic circle
   Antarctic circle
3. Latitude are measured in degrees
   Lines of latitude are shorter near the poles.
4. The longitude of a place is followed by the letter E for the east and W for west, 180 °E and 180 ° W is the same longitude called as international date line.
5. The point where the latitude and the longitude of a place intersect each other is the exact location of a place.

3 Movements of the Earth

A
1. Rotation-the earth spins on its axis from east to west which is called rotation and it causes day and night
2. Revolution-the earth moves around the sun in its orbit which is called revolution.
3. Axis-it is an imaginary line passing through the centre of the earth joining the poles
4. Orbit- the curved path in space that is followed by an object going round a planet

B
1. Axis 2. 24 hrs 3. Orbit
4. Axis 5. Rotation

C
1. c 2. d 3. e
4. a 5. b

D
1. All regions in the southern hemisphere experience summer during this time. this position of the earth is called summer solstice.
2. The direct rays of sun fall on the equator twice a year at this position neither of the poles are tilted towards the sun as a result the earth experiences equal day and nights which is called equinox

* These are suggested answers hence accept other valid answers too.

4 Continents and Oceans

C 1. Australia 2. Pacific 3. S shaped
4. India 5. Amazon

D 1. It is called an island continent as it is surrounded by water on all sides.
2. This continent is permanently covered with thick layer of ice hence it is called as frozen continent.
3. Africa is the home to deserts like Sahara and the Kalahari. It is the only continent through which tropic of cancer, tropic of Capricorn, equator and prime meridian pass.
4. Pacific Ocean and Atlantic Ocean
5. Ganga, Brahmaputra and the Indus.

5 Climatic Zones of the Earth

A 1. revolution 2. sea breeze
3. Torrid Zone 4. Frigid Zone
5. Tropic of Cancer, Arctic Circle

B 1. The distance from the equator and the latitude of a place , Altitude, distance from sea and direction of wind.
2. During day the land heats up faster than the sea, the air above becomes hot and rises up at that time cool air from sea rushes in to the vacuum created this is called sea breeze.
3. On the basis of latitude and overall climate patterns the world is divided into zones.
4. Weather is the condition of the atmosphere in one area at a particular time. Climate is a long-term prevalent weather condition of an area.
5. The frigid zone lies between Arctic Circle and north pole in the northern hemisphere and Antarctic Circle and south pole in the southern hemisphere, it receives slanted sunrays and low intensity of sun light as a result the area experience extreme cold climate.

6 The Equatorial Region

A 1. Emergent layer, canopy, understorey and forest floor
2. Gorillas, chimpanzees, monkeys, lemurs, bats, baboons and marmosets.
3. Rice, cassava and maize
4. Pygmies, Semangs and yanomano
5. Tropical climate with high temperature and humidity

B To be done by students

C 1. Species of tiny monkeys
2. A little amount spread in a small area
3. Something like a dead plant
4. A tribe from the DRC region
5. It is the crown of the trees

7 Temperate Grasslands

A 1. Temperate grasslands
2. Bison
3. Agriculture and livestock
4. Ranches.
5. Prairies

B 1. d 2. b 3. e
4. a 5. c

C 1. Corn, wheat, barley, oats and soya bean
2. Prairies extend from Canada to Mexico, the land is fertile, it has hot and wet summer and cold winter. It is called the wheat basket of the world; the major occupation is agriculture and cattle rearing.
3. The vegetation in the temperate grasslands primarily includes tall and short grasses. Tall grasses grow in areas that receive heavy rainfall, while short grasses grow in areas that have a continental climate. During autumn, the grasses wither and turn into hay. A few trees grow along the coasts in the southern temperate grasslands
4. The continental type of climate is characterized by hot summers cold winters and little rain fall.
5. Prairies has a surplus of wheat production which is exported to other nations hence it is called as wheat basket of the world.

8 Desert Region

A 1. b 2. e 3. d 4. a 5. c

C 1. KALAHARI 2. SAHARA
3. PATAGONIAN 4. MEXICAN
5. GOBI

D 1. Desert 2. Oasis
3. Camel 4. Great Victoria Desert
5. Gobi desert

9 Frigid Zone

A
1. North pole and Arctic Circle
2. South Pole and Antarctic Circle
3. Antarctica
4. Poles
5. North frigid zone

B
1. Name the countries that are located in the North frigid zone.

   Greenland, northern Canada, northern Alaska and northern Scandinavia
2. The Frigid Zones get less intense sunrays, which are spread over a wide area. These regions are covered with glaciers and a thick layer of ice called the ice cap. The climate here remains very cold throughout the year.

   There is continuous darkness during the winter and continuous daylight during the summer.
3. Yakuts, Samoyeds, Chukchis in Siberia, Aleuts in Alaska , Inuit in Greenland and Lapps in North scandinavia
4. Flower-bearing plants, shrubs bearing berries, mosses, lichens and grasses grow in the Frigid Zones
5. The animals that are normally found in these areas are wolves, foxes, voles, squirrels, snowshoe hare, musk ox, ermine, polar bears and reindeer.

ANSWER KEYS

Workbook Answers

1 Globes and Maps

Worksheet 1

A 1. bus station; 2. taxi stand; 3. light rail station; 4. train station; 5. airport; 6. swimming pool; 7. fast food; 8. food court; 9. cinema; 10. public toilet.

B 1. round; 2. axle; 3. scale; 4. intermediate directions; 5. conventional symbols.

C
1. A globe is a model of the Earth. It shows the distribution of water and land on Earth, and the correct shape and location of continents and oceans. A globe is useful when we want to study the Earth as a whole.
2. Maps are primarily of three kinds. (i) Physical maps show natural features of the Earth, such as mountains, plateaus, plains, rivers, oceans and other landforms and water bodies. (ii) Political maps show cities, towns and villages, and different countries and states of the world with their boundaries. (iii) Thematic maps focus on specific information, such as road maps, rainfall and distribution of natural vegetation, industries, minerals and many more.
3. Every map has a few specific components, namely scale, direction, signs and symbols, and colours known as the language of a map. (i) A scale is the ratio between the actual distance on the ground and the distance shown on the map. (ii) The four directions—north, south, east and west—are called cardinal directions. There are four sub-directions—north-east (ne), south-east (se), south-west (sw) and north-west (nw) which are called intermediate directions. (iii) Maps have a universal language of symbols. These are called conventional symbols. A table that lists the symbols used within the map and what they stand for is called a legend or a key. (iv) All maps use a standard colour scheme to depict various landforms and altitudes in maps.

Worksheet 2

Down – 1. scale; 2. globe; 3. physical; 4. thematic

Across – 3. political; 5. legend; 6. map

2 Latitudes and Longitudes

Worksheet

A Students will do themselves.

B Students will do themselves.

C
1. Latitudes and longitudes are imaginary lines that help us label every place on the surface of the earth. The most important line of latitude is the equator, which runs horizontally around the fattest part of the earth. The point where the latitude and the longitude of a place cut each other is the exact location of that place.
2. Longitudes help us to calculate the time of a place. We know that the Earth rotates on its axis. It completes one rotation in 24 hours or 1440 minutes. This means that it takes four minutes to rotate one degree. Each longitude is located at an interval of one degree. So, the time difference between two consecutive longitudes is four minutes. Therefore, if we know the longitude of a place we can also calculate the time of the place.
3. Coordinates like 15°N and 73°E show the exact location of Goa. They are the points where the latitude and the longitude of a place cut each other.

3 Movements of the Earth

A The pictures show different times of the day: morning, night caused by rotation of the Earth. The other set of pictures show summer and winter caused by revolution of the Earth.

B
1. Rotation
2. Because it is facing away from the Sun.

4 Continents and Oceans

Worksheet

A Students will do themselves.

B 1. hydrosphere; 2. lithosphere; 3. Bering Strait; 4. Eurasia; 5. frozen; 6. Australasia; 7. flora, fauna

5 Climatic Zones of the Earth

Worksheet 1

A
1. This is land breeze. As night falls, the land cools down faster than the sea. The warm air above the sea rises up and cooler air from the land rushes in to take its place.
2. This is sea breeze. During the day, the land heats up faster than the sea. The air above it becomes hot and being lighter than cold air, it rises up. The cool air that rushes in from the sea to fill the vacuum over the land is called sea breeze.

B Students will do themselves.

C 1. latitude; 2. altitude; 3. distance from the sea; 4. humidity; 5. direction of wind.

Worksheet 2

Across – 3. curvature; 6. altitude; 8. climate; 9. sea breeze.

Down – 1. humidity; 2. frigid; 4. land breeze; 5.seasons; 7. temperate

6 The Equatorial Region

Worksheet 1

Emergent layer; canopy layer; understorey; forest floor.

Worksheet 2

A
1. The equatorial region is located between the equator and the Tropic of Cancer (23½°N) in the Northern Hemisphere and between the equator and the Tropic of Capricorn (23½°S) in the Southern Hemisphere.
2. The equatorial region has a tropical climate with high temperatures and high humidity. The climate remains hot and wet throughout the year. The region receives direct rays of the Sun and has equal days and nights, and does not experience different seasons in a year. The accumulation of water droplets in the clouds throughout the day due to high temperature leads to heavy rainfall in the afternoon. This brings down the temperature, and makes the evenings and nights cooler.
3. The equatorial rainforests have a rich wildlife. Covering only 2 per cent of the Earth's surface, the rainforests are home to 10 per cent of the mammals and 20 per cent of the birds on the planet. Many species of mammals, including gorillas, chimpanzees, monkeys, lemurs, marmosets, flying squirrels, bats and baboons, reptiles such as crocodiles, alligators, snakes and lizards, and hippopotamus and jaguars are inhabitants of these forests. The rainforests also have an amazing population of birds, giraffes, antelopes and butterflies.
4. The Democratic Republic of the Congo shares its boundaries with Central African Republic and Sudan in the north; Tanzania, Burundi, Uganda and Rwanda in the east; Angola and Zambia in the south; and Republic of Congo in the west.

B Students will do themselves.

7 Temperate Grasslands

Worksheet 1

A 1. North America – Prairies; 2. South America – Pampas; 3. Africa – Veld; 4. Central Asia – Steppes; 5. Australia – Murray Darling Basin; 6. New Zealand – Canterbury plains

B 1. northern; southern; 2. extreme; moderate; 3. strong; 4. grazing; rodents; 5. Kirghiz; 6. Hottentots

Worksheet 2

Across – 1. Mississippi; 4. silos; 7.estancia; 8. Bison

Down – 2. Savannah; 3. Prairies; 5. ranch; 6. Kirghiz

8 Desert Region

Worksheet 1

A 1. T 2. F 3. T 4. F 5. T

B 1. Australia 2. Atacama, Patagonia
3. India 4. 50°

C 1. This is an oasis.

2. These are the only places in a desert where water and some vegetation can be found.

Worksheet 2

A 1. This is a picture depicting oil drills in deserts.
2. Saudi Arabia has rich deposits of oil.

B 1. Saudi Arabia is located in the hot desert region of the Arabian Peninsula. The Tropic of Cancer passes through the country. It is bound by the Red Sea in the west and the Persian Gulf in the east.
2. The country experiences a very hot and dry climate with little rainfall. The summer, which lasts from May to September, has extremely hot days and cool nights. During winter, from October to April, the days are warm and the nights are very cold.
3. The major occupation of the people is agriculture. Water for irrigation is obtained by desalting sea water. Wheat, rice, dates and alfalfa are the main crops. Tourism is a major source of income in the cities of Mecca and Medina. Saudi Arabia is rich in mineral resources, such as petroleum, which is the country's main source of income. Earlier, the people of Arabia led a nomadic lifestyle and did not have a fixed home. They moved from one place to another with their herds.

C 1. Camel　　2. Tuaregs
3. Bedouins　　4. wheat and barley

9 Frigid Zone

Worksheet 1

A 1. T　2. F　3. T　4. F　5. T

B 1. These people are called inuits.
2. They are the original inhabitants of Greenland.

C 1. North Canada　　2. North Alaska
3. North Scandinavia　　4. North Siberia

D 1. less intense　　2. once
3. Dwarf willow　　4. Caribou

Worksheet 2

A 1. Huskies are wolf-like dogs that are used for transportation.
2. Greenland is located to the north-east part of North America.
3. Greenland covers 21.5 lakh sq km.

B 1. This is the city of Nuuk.
2. It is located in Greenland.

C 1. Lapps　　2. Arctic Fox and Ermine
3. Nomadic hunting　　4. Inuits
5. Kayaks

Review Corner

A 1. thematic maps; 2. latitude; 3. Pangea; 4. north-south; 5. 23.5 degrees north.

B 1. true; 2. true; 3. false; 4. true; 5. true.

C 1. Drawing; it is not a composition of a map; 2. Space; it is not a type of pollution; 3. Eurasia; it is not an ocean; 4. Prime Meridian is not a parallel of latitude; 5. Red Sea: Its not an ocean

D 1. Directions are indicators on a map. The four directions—north, south, east and west—are called cardinal directions. Directions are an important part of a map. In most maps, you will find an arrow marked with the letter 'N' in the upper right hand corner, indicating the northern direction. It is called the north line. It is provided because when one knows the north direction, the rest of the directions can be found easily.
2. The imaginary lines running horizontal from east to west are called the parallels of latitude. The lines running vertically from north to south are called the meridians of longitude.
3. Oceans are important as they are home to a wide variety of marine life, which is a source of livelihood for many people around the world. Oceans have a moderating influence over the climate of coastal regions. Oceans also serve as a medium for transporting passengers and cargo through huge carrier ships.
4. While travelling satellites help tremendously. They help in navigation by picking up messages instantly and sending it to the receiver. The GPS system that we use today while travelling anywhere in the world is assisted by artificial satellites. They can pick up the location of a place and help in reaching the destination by following the correct route.

5. Lines of latitude and longitude are measured in degrees, and are noted by a directional compass letter, N, S, E, or W. Lines of longitude are perpendicular to lines of latitude, so they cross over, or intersect, whenever they meet. When locating a place on Earth, the intersection of a line of latitude and a line of longitude is used. To get a more accurate measurement of a location on Earth, degrees of latitude and longitude can be further divided into minutes and second. For each degree, there are 60 minutes, and each minute is divided into 60 seconds. Thus, a coordinate can be described in six digit terms, such as 27 58'48"N, 86 55'18"E for Mount Everest, Nepal.

Semester 2

1. Environmental Pollution

Textbook Reference: Pages 225–231 **Time Required: 9 periods**

Concepts

Four types of pollution, causes and solution, conservation of environment, 3Rs

Teaching materials

Pictures, things made from biodegradable materials, charts and videos

Learning Outcomes

After this lesson, students will be able to:

- Explaining the causes of pollution
- Know the steps to be taken to control pollution
- Learn the need of conservation
- Explain the importance of 3Rs

Periods	Methodology	Assess
Period 1 **Concept** Environmental pollution, 3Rs	Teacher talks about the natural resources available for mankind and how man is responsible for the pollution caused. She keeps four sample bins on the table and explains the concept of the 3Rs i.e. reduce, reuse and recycle. Ask students to answer the questions in **Take off** and **Warm up.**	• Name the kinds of pollutions.
Period 2 and 3 **Concept** Air pollution, water pollution, soil pollution	The students are asked to take a deep breath and are asked to say whether they were able to smell something nice, students give varied answers then the teacher explains about the causes of air pollution. She further asks them to see two glasses of water on table one is pure and the other is impure. She explains the water pollution causes and solution. The teacher explains the water pollution. soil pollution is explained with a help of a video when students make noise, teacher points out the noise pollution.	• How does air pollution affect us? • How Is water polluted? • Why soil should be protected from pollution and how?

Period 4 **Concept** Conserve the environment	How to conserve the environment? Students come forward with lot of suggestions and the teacher summarize the answer and writes the same on the board. Conservation means saving and protecting the environment. Our environment is a storehouse of natural resources.	• Students are asked to write a slogan on conservation of environment. • Create flashcards on the four types of pollution.
Period 5 Summary	Find out the various steps that you can take to prevent environmental pollution. Group discussion is made on the above topic. **Summary** Teacher explains about the 3Rs which are the foundational principles of conservation of natural resources and energy. **Recall** A flowchart is made on the board to recall all the key points.	• Each group is asked to make bins for collecting paper, metal, glass and plastic asked to make a poster on save earth.
Period 6	Ask students to complete the activities and answer the questions in **Do It Yourself**, **Find out**, **Think** and **Enjoy**.	
Period 7	Ask the students to answer the questions in **Work out**.	

2. Evolution of Transport and Communication

Textbook Reference: Pages 232–237 | **Time Required: 8 periods**

Concepts

Transport, land, air, water transport, communication, media and internet

Teaching Materials

Pictures, video clippings, course book

Learning Outcomes

After this lesson, students will be able to:

- Know importance of the inventions
- Know the advantages of the inventions
- Take pride in the contributions of the inventors

Periods	Methodology	Assess
Period 1 and 2 **Concept** Revolutionary changes	The teacher asks students about the use of wheels and narrates the story of its invention. The wheel led to the coming of steam engine. The invention of the wheel brought a revolutionary change in the way early humans travelled. Ask students to answer the questions in **Take off** and **Warm up**. Advancements in science and technology have led to easier and faster means of transportation; teacher now shows the picture of various types of transport and communication and explains each in detail.	• Name the inventions in transport. • Name the fastest trains in the world. • Name the road linking India and Pakistan. • Name the three types of ships.
Period 3 and 4 **Concepts** Railway network, ships, waterways, air ways	Railways are an important means of transport. Ports can be river ports and seaports and they house a great variety of ships. Special ships called oil tankers are used to transport oil. Refrigerated ships are used to transport vegetables, fruits, meat and dairy products. Cruise ships ferry passengers around the world. Aeroplanes have become faster and capable of carrying huge amounts of cargo and hundreds of passengers at a time.	• Name the fastest mode of transport. • In what way newspapers are useful to us.

Period 5 and 6 **Concepts** Printing press, internet, newspapers, magazines, radio, films, media	With this invention, the printing of books was initiated. The Internet is by far the fastest means of communication. Nowadays, wireless mobile or cellular phones are used to send messages and speak to people all around the world. Newspapers and magazines or journals help to gain knowledge about the different events occurring around the world. Radio relays information and entertains people. It is an auditory medium Television is one of the most popular means of mass communication. Film or cinema is another audio-visual means of mass communication to educate and entertain people through cinema. **Summary** Teacher asks students to learn to protect all the facilities and not misuse them.	**Group Activity** • Design a newspaper of your class. • How does film help in education?
Period 7	Ask students to complete the activities and answer the questions in **Do It Yourself**, **Find out**, **Think** and **Enjoy**.	
Period 8	Ask the students to answer the questions in **Work out**.	

3. India Over the Ages

Textbook Reference: Pages 238–244 **Time Required: 7 periods**

Concepts

Three periods of history of India, ancient, medieval and modern period, iron age of India, rise of empire, British rule

Teaching Materials

Maps, atlas, pictures, videos

Learning Outcomes

After this lesson, students will be able to:

- Learn about the Indus Valley and Aryan Civilization
- Understand the contributions of the rulers
- Learn the reasons for the arrival of British in India
- Learn about the leaders of India and their contributions

Periods	Methodology	Assess
Period 1 **Concept** Three periods of the history of India	The teacher introduces the topic. The history of India is divided into three periods—the ancient period, the medieval period and the modern period. During each of these periods, India had different inhabitants and different rulers too. Ask students to answer the questions in **Take off** and **Warm up.**	• The history of India is divided into _______ , _______ and _______ period.
Period 2 **Concept** Ancient	The ancient period saw the rise of the Indus Valley Civilization, the coming of the Indo-Aryans and the rise of empires in India. During the Vedic Period, sixteen kingdoms existed in India. These were small tribes or mahajanapadas.	• Name the sixteen Mahajanapadas. • Name the famous king famous king of the Mauryan period.

Period 3 **Concept** Iron age of India, Rise of Empires	Magadha emerged as the most powerful mahajanapada. The Mauryan Empire was one of the most powerful empire. Ashoka the Great, was one of the greatest Indian kings, He adopted a policy of non-violence. The Gupta Empire was another great empire of ancient India the immense developments made during this period in the fields of science, medicine, literature, language and astronomy.	• Mention the contributions of the Gupta rulers.
Period 3 and 4 **Concept** Medieval	The Delhi Sultanate and the Mughal Empire are the two major kingdoms during the medieval period. The Mughal Empire was established by Babur who came to India from Central Asia. Some of the notable rulers of the Mughal period were Akbar, Shah Jahan and Aurangzeb. In the south, the Vijayanagara Empire was most powerful. Krishnadevaraya was the most remarkable ruler of this empire.	• Name the rulers of the Delhi Sultanate. • What was the contribution of Mughals to art and architecture? • Who was the famous king of the Vijayanagar Empire?
Period 5 **Concepts** Modern period, British rule	The British began their journey in India as a small trading company known as the East India Company**,** which eventually took control of the country. The British ruled India for 200 years. The teacher draws a flowchart and shows the growth of kingdoms.	• Mention buildings constructed by Britishers in India. **Activity** Mark the dynasties in the given map. Make a chart of the monuments built by Akbar the Great.
Period 6	Ask students to complete the activities and answer the questions in **Do It Yourself**, **Find out**, **Think** and **Enjoy**.	
Period 7	Ask the students to answer the questions in **Work out**.	

4. British Period in India

Textbook Reference: Pages 245–250 **Time Required: 9 periods**

Concepts

Discovery of sea route, establishment of East India Company, Battle of Plassey, Battle of Buxar, discontent against the British

Teaching Materials

Course book, maps, pictures, videos

Learning Outcomes

After this lesson, students will be able to:

- Explain that the sea route opened new trade relations
- Learn that disunity among Indian rulers had caused the entry of Britishers
- Understand the richness of our Nation

Periods	Methodology	Assess
Period 1 **Concept** Discovery of sea route	Teacher poses a question How do people develop trade relation? What are the ways? Further explains that the discovery of the sea route to India via the Cape of Good Hope by the Portuguese explorer, Vasco da Gama, in 1498 opened up new doors for merchants and traders in India and Europe. Ask students to answer the questions in **Take off** and **Warm up.**	• Who discovered the sea route and when?
Period 2 **Concepts** New opening for trade, establishment of the East India Company	Trade between India and European countries like the Netherlands, France and Great Britain flourished. In 1600 CE, the British established their company called the East India Company. The British emerged victorious and went on to control most of the trade in India.	• When did the Britishers establish the Company?

Period 3 and 4 **Concept** Battle of Plassey, Battle of Buxar	Since no permission was taken from Siraj-ud-Daulah, the then Nawab of Bengal, the Battle of Plassey took place in 1757 between the Nawab's army and the British.The British were able to consolidate themselves in Bengal by removing Siraj-ud- Daulah and making Mir Jafar, a puppet of the British, the Nawab.	• Who was the Bengal ruler who refused permission to Britishers?
Period 5 and 6 **Concept** Discontent against the British, Revolt of 1857	Why were the Indians unhappy Do you know? As soon as the East India Company gained control over India, they started exploiting the people, As a result of their growing discontent, the people of India decided to revolt against the British. This rebellion is called the Revolt of 1857. The revolt brought about several changes. The British government took control over the administration of the country, bringing the rule of the East India Company to an end. Queen Victoria became the Empress of India.	• What made Indians unhappy with Britishers? • When and where did the revolt start? • Name the Indian rulers who took part in the revolt.
Period 7 **Concept** Social reforms	The educated Indians worked towards social reforms. In 1885, AO Hume founded the Indian National Congress (INC). It aimed at involving the educated Indians in the country's administration Teacher summarizes the lesson in the form a narration	• Name the social reformers. • Who founded the INC and when? • Activity • Mark the sea route. • Place where the battles took place. • Place where the Company was established.
Period 8	Ask students to complete the activities and answer the questions in **Do It Yourself**, **Find out**, **Think** and **Enjoy**.	
Period 9	Ask the students to answer the questions in **Work out**.	

5. Attaining Freedom

Textbook Reference: Pages 251–256 **Time Required: 8 periods**

Concepts

Divide and rule, Partition of Bengal, Swadeshi Movement, Satyagraha, Jallianwala Massacre, Dandi March

Teaching Materials

Movie on the freedom struggle, pictures, maps, charts

Learning Outcomes

After this lesson, students will be able to:

- Learn the struggle of the freedom fighters
- Understand the non-violent steps taken to fight for freedom
- Learn the importance of using Indian materials to encourage our workers

Periods	Methodology	Assess
Period 1 **Concepts** Divide and rule, Partition of Bengal	Teacher explains the reason of divide and rule policy and proceeds. The Partition of Bengal was devised by the British to achieve this motive. They decided to divide the Bengal province based on religion. Ask students to answer the questions in **Take off** and **Warm up.**	• When was the partition of Bengal devised?
Period 2 and 3 **Concepts** Swadeshi movement, Satyagraha	People took part in several strikes and protests, boycotting goods made by the British and even burning them. This movement was called the Swadeshi Movement. The British tried to suppress the movement but by that time it had spread to all parts of the country. Gandhi assumed the leadership of Indian National Congress and led nationwide non-violent protests or Satyagraha against the oppressive British rule.	• What is Swadeshi movement? • What is the meaning of Satyagraha? • Locate Jallianwala Bagh on a map.

Period 4 **Concept** Jallianwala Massacre, Dandi March	Thousands of people gathered at the Jallianwala Bagh in Amritsar for a peaceful protest. However, the British blocked the exit and opened fire on the gathering, killing and injuring many people. This was a turning point in India's fight for freedom. Outraged by the indiscriminate killing, Gandhi encouraged people to follow complete disobedience and non-cooperation with the British. Gandhiji urged people to produce salt without paying any tax.	• Why did Gandhiji start Dandi March? • Name the leaders involved in the struggle for freedom.
Period 5 and 6 **Concept** INA, attaining freedom	Subhash Chandra Bose formed the Indian National Army. India became free on 15 August 1947. The country was, however, divided into two separate nations—India and Pakistan. Dr Rajendra Prasad was the first President of India and Jawaharlal Nehru was elected as the first Prime Minister of India **Activity** Make a chart with the pictures of our Indian leaders.	• When did India get freedom? • Draw and colour the national flag.
Period 7	Ask students to complete the activities and answer the questions in **Do It Yourself**, **Find out**, **Think** and **Enjoy**.	
Period 8	Ask the students to answer the questions in **Work out**.	

6. Indian Government

Textbook Reference: Pages 257–262 **Time Required: 11 periods**

Concepts

Constitution, central government, state government, judiciary, legislature, executive, parliament and two houses, president, prime minister

Teaching Materials

Pictures, course book, charts

Learning Outcomes

After this lesson, students will be able to:
- Learn the need of constitution
- Know the purpose of Government and its work
- Learn and comprehend the functions of the three wings of the government

Periods	Methodology	Assess
Period 1 **Concept** Constitution	Teacher asks a question. Why do we need the rules and law? What if we do not have rules? A discussion is done and teacher proceeds talking about the constitution. Ask students to answer the questions in **Take off** and **Warm up.**	Define the term constitution.
Period 2 and 3 **Concept** Central and state governments	The Constitution of India provides for a single central government and state governments for each state. Power is shared between the states and the Centre. The central government governs the entire country. It makes the laws that are applicable to everyone in the country. The state governments maintain the law and order in their respective states.	• What is the role of the central government? • Name the three wings of the government.

Period 4 **Concepts** Judiciary, legislature and executive	The central government has three branches: the legislature, the executive and the judiciary. The parliament or the legislature makes laws. The executive, consisting of the President and his appointed officers, implements the laws. The judiciary ensures that laws are not violated.	• What is the role of the legislature?
Period 5 and 6 **Concepts** Parliament and two houses	The Lok Sabha is also called the House of the People since it comprises members who have been directly elected by the people of India. It is also known as the Lower House. The Rajya Sabha is the Upper House of the Parliament. The members of the Rajya Sabha are chosen by members of the state legislative assemblies	• Name the two houses of the parliament. • What is the power of the President of India? • Name the state assembly.
Period 7 **Concepts** President and prime minister	The President is the head of the country and the supreme commander of the armed forces. This leader becomes the Prime Minister of the country.	• Who is the head of the state?
Period 8 **Concept** State assembly	The state legislative assembly is also known as the Vidhan Sabha. The legislative assembly makes laws for the state. The leader of this party is chosen as the Chief Minister, The head of a state is a Governor. The High Court is the highest judicial authority in a state or a union territory.	
Period 9 **Concept** Judiciary	The Supreme Court of India is the highest judicial body in India. It has the final say in all legal matters, Teacher recalls all the key points in a flowchart.	• Name the highest judicial authority in state.
Period 10	Ask students to complete the activities and answer the questions in **Do It Yourself**, **Find out**, **Think** and **Enjoy**.	
Period 11	Ask the students to answer the questions in **Work out**.	

7. United Nations

Textbook Reference: Pages 263–268 **Time Required: 8 periods**

Concepts

World War, formation of the UN, six organs of the UN, special agencies of the UN, India and the UN

Teaching Materials

Chart, pictures, newspapers

Learning Outcomes

After this lesson, students will be able to:

- Comprehend the role and responsibility of the UN
- Comprehend the need of specialized agencies
- Understand the need of world peace

Periods	Methodology	Assess
Period 1 **Concepts** World War, formation of the UN	Teacher narrates the story of World War and informs that many people were killed hence the need for an organization came up and that is how UN was born. Ask students to answer the questions in **Take off** and **Warm up.**	• When was the UN created?
Period 2, 3 and 4 **Concepts** The six organs of the UN	The membership to the UN is open to all peace-loving states. The main objectives of the UN are: To maintain peace in the world. The **General Assembly** is the main body of the UN. It deals with important global issues. The **Security Council** maintains global peace and security. The **Economic and Social Council** looks after the economic, **humanitarian**, social and cultural activities	• Who can become the member? • What are the objectives of UN?

<table>
<tr><td>Period 5 and 6

Concept
India and UN, the special agencies of the UN, role of India</td><td>The Trusteeship Council was created to look after these nations. The International Court of Justice is the judicial body. It deals with international legal issues and advises countries on international legal matters. The Secretariat deals with the daily activities of the UN.

Special agencies are:

Teacher discusses the role of these agencies.
UNESCO
UNICEF
ILO
FAO
WHO

Role of India

India became a member of the UN on 30 October 1945. As one of the founding members, India strongly supports the purposes and programmes of the UN. It has made significant contributions in the United Nations peacekeeping.

Activity

Group work in listing the work of the UN organs and special agencies.</td><td>• How many organs does the UN have?
• How many specialized agencies are there?
• Draw the emblem of UN.
• Draw the flag of the UN.</td></tr>
<tr><td>Period 7</td><td>Ask students to complete the activities and answer the questions in Do It Yourself, Find out, Think and Enjoy.</td><td></td></tr>
<tr><td>Period 8</td><td>Ask the students to answer the questions in Work out.</td><td></td></tr>
</table>

Values Corner

Textbook Reference: Pages 274–275 **Time Required: 2 periods**

TOLERANCE

Concepts

Tolerance, belief, customs, culture

Teaching Materials

Story, chart, pictures

Learning Outcomes

- Learn to define tolerance
- Learn its importance and effects
- Know that tolerance builds relationship

Concepts	Methodology	Assessment
Meaning of tolerance	Start with a story of leaders who are tolerant towards people. Ask the students are asked few questions: Why should the leaders tolerate the public attitude?	Define tolerance.
Attitude	What will happen if we do not tolerate certain behavior of people? Students give their answers and the teacher explains the purpose of being tolerant.	Why should we be tolerant?
Unhappy	If we don't develop this attitude, then we may end in quarrel and unhappy situations.	What will happen if we are not tolerant?
Beliefs	Beliefs, or practices, of others that differ from one's own. No culture is good or bad. We should never try to force our beliefs or customs on others.	Make a poster with quotes related to tolerance.

Culture	Teacher further informs students to be friendly with all, learn to be calm and not to express anger or displeasure to anyone. **Group Activity** Write a short skit on tolerance.	Complete the activity given in the value card.

ACCEPTANCE

Concepts

Acceptance, happiness, friendly, praise

Teaching Materials

Pictures, charts, video clippings, story book/ story chart

Learning Outcomes

- Define the term acceptance
- Learn the impact of acceptance
- Learn that happiness depends on accepting people and situations
- Learn to praise and appreciate people

Concepts	Methodology	Assessment
Acceptance	*Happiness can only exist in acceptance.*	What makes us happy?
Happiness	Explain to the students that acceptance of someone into our group means we are beginning to think of them as part of our group and to act in a friendly way towards them.	Why we should praise people?
Praise	Everyone is good at something. We must learn to praise everyone for their help and support. Ask the students to share incidence where they showed acceptance.	
Appreciate	Ask students to share events when they had appreciated people for their good work.	How do people feel when we appreciatethem?
Criticize	Inform students that we must praise everyone for their work and must not criticize or make fun of them.	How do people feel when we criticize them?

Activity	**Group Activity** Make an emblem for acceptance with a slogan. Complete the exercise given in the value card.	Make a happy face with a paper plate and put it in the class.

INITIATIVE

Concepts

Taking Initiative, ability to do, not dependent, learn new things

Teaching Materials

- Story of great achievers
- Film on people who take initiatives
- Pictures and chart

Learning Outcomes

- Understand the meaning of initiative
- Comprehend the need of ability for skills
- Understand the need of being independent

Concepts	Methodology	Assessment
Need of initiative	Tell the student to write the topic on the board and waits for someone to come forward. When someone comes, say that this act is called initiative further she explains that initiative is the ability to decide what to do next without needing other people to tell you what to do.	What is initiative?
Taking Initiative	Read a story and shows how the move to help or to do something is called an initiative.	Have you tried to help anyone?
Ability to do	Ask the students to take the initiative to learn something new every day.	Did you try to learn new things?
Not dependent	Be more forthcoming and help people. What will you do when someone wants a help? What will you do when students disturb the class? Will you keep watching or move to help.	Ask the students to speak about the things they have learnt.

Learn new things	Inform the students to take initiative in learning new skills and not to be dependent, only this act can make people develop ability to learn and do.	Take a Stand A group of children are spoiling public property. Write what you would say to them.

LOYALTY

Concepts

Loyalty, faithful, friendship, being firm, supportive

Teaching Materials

Stories of leaders of the nation, pictures of great leaders, chart, video clippings

Learning Outcomes

- Understand the meaning of loyalty
- Learn to be faithful
- Support friends and take firm decision

Concepts	Methodology	Assessment
Loyalty	Define the term loyalty. It is the devotion and faithfulness to a nation.	Define loyalty.
Being loyal	Inform that loyalty is the quality of staying firm in your friendship or give support for someone. Loyalty is being faithful to people, country or ideas. We should be supportive to the people who are loyal to us.	In what way you would express your loyalty towards the nation?
Faithful	Ask these questions: Did you share your notes with your friend who was absent yesterday? Did you attend the Independence Day celebration?	Have you ever helped your friend in distress? Compete the activity given in the value card.
Friendship	Ask the students to share an incident at home or school where they had shown faithful work or supported their friends in any form.	Share a story or read a story about loyalty.

Being firm	**Activity** Ask the students to write a skit on loyalty.	Write a quote on loyalty.
Supportive	**Individual Activity** Ask the students to make a placard with message of loyalty and faithfulness. Ask the students to speak truth. Be firm in taking decisions and loyal to the school and society.	

1. ENVIRONMENTAL POLLUTION

A Answer these questions.

1. What are the four main causes of pollution?
2. How is the ozone layer affected by pollution?
3. What causes soil pollution?
4. What causes noise pollution?

B Match the following.

Column A	Column B
1. Noise pollution	a. Garbage
2. Soil pollution	b. Depletion
3. Water pollution	c. Smoke
4. Air pollution	d. Honking
5. Ozone layer	e. Chemicals

C Draw and colour four types of recycle bins.

D Make a chart on 'Save the earth' slogan.

Name: .... Teacher's signature: ....

Class: .... Date: ....

2. EVOLUTION OF TRANSPORT AND COMMUNICATION

A Name the inventors of these inventions.

1. Steam engine ....
2. Radio ....
3. Television ....
4. Telegraph machine ....
5. Telephone ....

B Match the following.

	Column A		Column B
1.	Grand Trunk Road	a.	Aeroplanes
2.	Printing Press	b.	Radio
3.	Wright brothers	c.	India
4.	Cruise ships	d.	Johannes Gutenberg
5.	Marconi	e.	Ferry passengers

C Write the year of invention.

1. Telephone ....
2. Radio ....
3. Television ....
4. Printing Press ....
5. Aeroplane ....

D Answer these questions.

1. How did the early man communicate?
2. Write a short note on the railway network.
3. How does cinema help in communication?
4. What were the problems faced before the printing press was invented?
5. Name the types of ships used for transport.

Name: .... Teacher's signature: ....

Class: .... Date: ....

3. INDIA OVER THE AGES

A Fill in the blanks.

1. Victoria Memorial was built by ....
2. .... was the famous ruler of the Vijayanagara Empire.
3. The Mughal Empire was founded by ....
4. The .... and the .... are the two major kingdoms of the medieval period.
5. .... emerged as the most powerful mahajanapada.

B Match the following.

	Column A		Column B
1.	Shahjahan	a.	Mauryan ruler
2.	Aryans	b.	Vijayanagara empire
3.	Hampi	c.	Golden period
4.	Gupta rule	d.	Mughal ruler
5.	Ashoka	e.	Central Asia

C Identify the monuments and write who constructed them.

1. 

....

....

2. 

....

....

3. 

....

....

4. 

....

....

5. 

....

....

Name: .... Teacher's signature: ....

Class: .... Date: ....

4. BRITISH PERIOD IN INDIA

A **Mention the year in which these events occurred.**

1. Battle of Plassey .... 2. Battle of Buxar ....
3. First War of Indian Independence ....
4. Formation of the Indian National Congress ....

B **Match the following.**

	Column A		Column B
1.	Dayanand Saraswathi	a.	Nawab of Bengal
2.	Rani Lakshmibai	b.	Reformer
3.	Tantia Tope	c.	Jhansi
4.	Siraj-ud-Daulah	d.	Kanpur

C **Answer these questions.**

1. Name some prominent members of the Indian National Congress.
2. Mention a few social reforms brought by the reformers.
3. What was the impact of the new sea route discovery?
4. Who started the Revolt of 1857 and where?
5. What was the aim of the Indian National Congress?

D **Identify the people in the pictures.**

....

Name: .... Teacher's signature: ....

Class: .... Date: ....

5. ATTAINING FREEDOM

A Answer these questions.

1. Name the three reformers who revolted against the Partition of Bengal.
2. What was the Partition of Bengal?
3. Describe the Jallianwala Bagh massacre.
4. What is Dandi March?
5. What is Satyagraha?

B Fill in the blanks.

1. The British followed the policy of ....
2. The boycotting of the British goods was the aim of .... movement.
3. Gandhiji led a nationwide non-violent protest called ....
4. .... means total independence.
5. Salt satyagraha is also called as ....

C Fill the year of the event correctly.

1. Dandi March ....
2. Partition of Bengal ....
3. Formation of INA ....
4. India gained independence ....
5. Jallianwala Bagh massacre ....

D Identify the persons in the picture and list their contributions if the freedom struggle.

....

....

....

....

....

....

....

Name: .... Teacher's signature: ....

Class: .... Date: ....

6. INDIAN GOVERNMENT

A Fill in the blanks.

1. The .... contains the rules and laws that govern the citizen of the nation.
2. The .... governs the entire country.
3. The legislature makes ....
4. The .... is also called the House of the People
5. The Lok Sabha is presided by the ....

B Match the following.

Column A	Column B
1. Judiciary	a. Highest judicial body
2. Rajya Sabha	b. State assembly
3. Constitution	c. Upper house
4. Vidhan Sabha	d. Rules and laws
5. Supreme Court	e. Protects law

C Answer in one word.

1. Head of the state ....
2. Leader of the state elected Party ....
3. Head of the country ....
4. Chairman of Rajya Sabha ....
5. Presiding officer of Lok Sabha ....

Name: .... Teacher's signature: ....

Class: .... Date: ....

7. UNITED NATIONS

A Fill in the blanks.

1. The work of UN is carried out by .... main organs.
2. The main objective of UN is to maintain .... in the world.
3. .... was the first Secretary General of the UN.
4. The International Court of Justice is the judicial body of the UN is located at .... in Netherlands.
5. The Secretary General of the UN heads the ....

B Write the full forms of these UN special agencies.

1. UNESCO ....
2. WHO ....
3. UNICEF ....
4. ILO ....
5. FAO ....

C Answer these questions.

1. Write a short note on the Security Council.
2. Who can be the member of the UN?
3. What is the work of Economic and Social Council?
4. What is the purpose of FAO?
5. Write a note on the relationship between UN and India.

D Draw and colour the UN flag and emblem.

Name: .... Teacher's signature: ....

Class: .... Date: ....

Coursebook Answers

1 Environmental Pollution

Take off

- We breathe in air.
- Smoke makes the air polluted.

Warm up

The people are bathing and washing their vegetables in the river. No, the river is not clean.

Workout

A 1. a. 2. a. 3. a. 4. b.

B 1. ozone 2. noise pollution 3. fossil fuels 4. non-biodegradable

C 1. T 2. F 3. T 4. F 5. T

D

1. Air pollution happens when harmful gases and other pollutants enter the atmosphere.
2. Water pollution can lead to diseases such as cancer, skin diseases, stomach ailments, etc. among humans. It can also lead to the death of marine animals and plant life.
3. Non-biodegradable waste is something that cannot be broken down by bacteria. Non-biodegradable waste stops organisms that live inside the soil from getting the oxygen that they need.
4. Noise pollution is when there is too much unpleasant noise in the environment caused by horns, cars, firecrackers and loud music.
5. Air pollution happens mostly because of human made reasons. One of the major reasons of air pollution is the poisonous gases and smoke that are emitted by cars and chimneys of factories. The firecrackers burst during Diwali emanate smoke and pollute the air. When wood, coal, dry leaves and kerosene are burnt it leads to air pollution as well. Deforestation, or cutting down of trees, is also one major reason for air pollution.
   The major reason for water pollution is throwing of waste into the same. Chemicals, oils and toxic waste dumped into water bodies by companies – as well as leaking of oil tankers – can lead to water pollution as well. When agricultural waste is thrown in the sea it can lead to water pollution. Often pesticides and fertilizers seep into groundwater through the soil. This can lead to water pollution as well.
6. Air pollution can lead to breathing problems and as such is rather harmful for all living beings. When air gets polluted humans and animals can become sick. Air pollution can also lead to global warming and climate change. When gases and other harmful substances increase in the atmosphere the temperature of that place increases as well and the climate of that place changes as a whole. Air pollution can also lead to acid rain. Harmful substances are given out when fossil fuels burn. These substances mix with water particles and lead to a form of rain that is also known as acid rain. They may fall down as snow as well and damage forests, soils, water bodies and buildings. Air pollution also affects the ozone layer, which saves us from the harmful UV rays of the Sun.
   When people drink polluted water and swim in that it can lead to diseases such as cancer, stomach problems and skin diseases. Marine animals such as fishes die when water is polluted. Water pollution also entails other kinds of risks for plants in seas and oceans.
7. We can reduce noise pollution by using vehicle horns as less as possible and not play music loudly. Use of firecrackers should also be avoided.
8. Recycling, reduce water consumption, reduce the use of electricity, plant a tree, grow vegetables, composting, use rechargeable batteries and many more ways to conserve the environment.
9. The three R's are reduce, reuse and recycle. They can help us conserve natural resources and protect the environment.

* These are suggested answers hence accept other valid answers too.

Think

A There are some basic steps, which if taken, will help in stopping environmental pollution. First of all, people need to plant more trees, use harmful substances like fossil fuels and pesticides as little as possible. Waste should be thrown at places that are specifically designated for the purpose. It is also important to obey the laws related to pollution like not blowing horns, not listening to high pitch music, and not bursting sound based crackers, etc.*

Life skills and values

The first thing to do is to stop using plastic bags and then throwing them away once they have been used. It is also important to monitor cows when they are grazing.*

2 Evolution of Transport and Communication

Take off

- The invention of the wheel made travelling easy.
- Bullock carts were used to travel.

Warm up

Hot air balloon; it is used for recreational purposes where passengers get to see places from extremely high altitudes.

Find out

Grand Trunk Road was built buy Sher Shah Suri and was known as Shah Rah-e-Azam.

Do it yourself*

Port	Port of Shanghai	Singapore
Country	China	Singapore

Port	Shenzhen	Hong Kong	Busan
Country	China	China	South Korea

Workout

A 1. a. 2. a. 3. c. 4. a.

B 1. Shinkansen 2. refrigerated ships 3. Amazon 4. airways

C 1. T 2. F 3. F 4. T

D
1. James Watt invented the steam engine.
2. A highway is any public or private road or other public way on land. It is used for major roads, but also includes other public roads and public tracks
3. Shanghai Maglev, Shinkansen
4. Mississippi river, Danube and Ganges.
5. The Wright Brothers invented the first aeroplane.
6. The fastest mode of communication is through the use of a telephone.

Think

1. Steamer
2. To take people from one place to another

Life skills and values

Without aeroplanes or cars, early humans either walked or rode on horses or bullock carts to travel from one place to another. This meant more travel time for the people making it less safe to travel to far off places.*

Enjoy

The Grand Trunk Road is the oldest road in India.

3 India Over the Ages

Take off

- History is the study of the past.
- People who study history and write about it are called historians.

Warm up

Qutb Minar, Delhi

Find out

Valmiki

Do it yourself

1. The pictures shows Rashtrapati Bhavan.
2. It is located in Delhi.
3. It was built by the British.

Workout

A 1. a. 2. c. 3. b. 4. b. 5. a.

B 1. Akbar 2. Babur 3. Aryans 4. East India Company

C 1. T 2. T 3. T 4. T

D
1. Fatehpur Sikri was built during the Mughal era by emperor Akbar.
2. The rule of Gupta dynasty is also known as the Golden Age of India.
3. Aryans or Vedic civilization used iron.
4. The famous emperor of the Vijayanagara Empire was Krishnadeva Raya.
5. During the medieval period, the Turks invaded several parts of India and established their rule. Several powerful dynasties ruled over India. The Delhi Sultanate was established by Qutb-ud-Din Aibak. The powerful dynasties that ruled during this time are the Tughlaq Dynasty, the Sayyid Dynasty and the Lodhi Dynasty. The Lodis were deposed by Babur who established Mughal rule in India. Several great monarchs, such as Akbar, Shah Jahan and Aurangzeb ruled Delhi during this period. In the south, Krishnadeva Raya was a famous ruler of the Vijayanagara Empire. Several monuments near Hampi in Karnataka were built during the Vijayanagara Empire and now they serve as the source of information about the architecture of this empire. Some of the famous monuments built during this period are the famous Taj Mahal, the Red Fort, the Shalimar Gardens, the Jama Masjid, Fatehpur Sikri and the Buland Darwaza amongst many others.
6. After the Indus Valley Civilization declined, a new group of people came to India from Central Asia during 1500 BCE. They were called the Aryans. Their religion was later known as Hinduism and they spoke Sanskrit. They learnt the use of iron and began to make tools. They domesticated the horse. We can learn about the Aryans from the four Vedas and epics like the Ramayana and Mahabharata. The Bhagwad Gita, which is the most sacred text of the Hindus, is part of the Mahabharata.
7. The British built many historical monuments in India. Some of them are the Victoria Memorial, the Gateway of India, Fort St George, the Chhatrapati Shivaji Terminus and the monuments that surround Lutyens Delhi like India Gate and the Rashtrapati Bhavan.

Think
1. Lion Capital of Ashoka
2. India
3. Currency notes/Indian rupee

4 British Period in India

Take off
- The British ruled India for 200 years.
- Freedom fighters like Mahatma Gandhi helped India gain independence.

Warm up
The British reached India on ship.

Do it yourself

Country	Great Britain	France
Company name	English East India Company	French East India Company
Base place	Kolkata	Pondicherry and Chandernagore

Portugal	The Netherlands
Companhia do commércio da Índia	Dutch East India Company
Goa	Malabar

Find out
British territorial aggression and their new policies like land revenue rules, introduction of railways and telegraphs only led to discontent among the Indians who thought these to be interference in their lives. Dalhousie's policy of doctrine of lapse by which many Indian rulers were deposed also led them to band together to fight the British.*

Workout
A 1. a. 2. a. 3. a. 4. c. 5. b.

B 1. Queen Victoria 2. Rani of Jhansi
3. Indian National Congress
4. Raja Rammohan Roy*

C 1. T 2. F 3. T 4. F 5. T

D
1. Vasco da Gama was the Portuguese explorer who found the sea route to India.
2. The British established trading centres in Bombay and Madras. Although they obtained permission from the Mughal emperors, no permission was taken from the Nawab of Bengal, Siraj-ud-Daulah.
3. Apart from the British, the French, the Portuguese and the Dutch traded with India.
4. The Indians were not happy during British rule since they were being exploited by the British.

5. The Indian National Congress was formed in order to get educated Indians involved in the political administration.
7. The Indian leaders who took part in the revolt were Rani Lakshmibai of Jhansi, Nana Saheb and Tantia Tope in Kanpur, Begum Hazrat Mahal in Awadh, Maulavi Ahmadullah, Rao Tula Ram and Kunwar Singh.
8. Raja Ram Mohan Roy and Syed Ahmad Khan

Think

The common people who depended on food crops would be affected the most when the Indian farmers were asked to grow cash crops instead of food crops.*

Life skills and values

With the introduction of western education people gained greater knowledge and understanding of concepts like liberty and freedom. They realized that the British had no right to keep them enslaved. The introduction of railways helped people from various classes and parts of country come together and interact. This helped Indians realize that their strength lay in unity – this realization served as the bedrock of the national independence movement.*

5 Attaining Freedom

Take off

- The British introduced modern education in India.
- The Indian National Congress was formed in 1885.

Warm up

Bhagat Singh

He is one of India's leading freedom fighters.

Find out

Mahatma Gandhi, Jawaharlal Nehru, Vallabhbhai Patel and prominent congress leaders were arrested at on set of Quit India Movement.

Do it yourself

The first INA was formed by Rash Behari Bose during 1942.

Workout

A 1. a. 2. a. 3. b 4. c. 5. c.

B 1. Divide and rule 2. Satyagraha movement 3. Dandi 4. Dr Rajendra Prasad

C 1. T 2. F 3. T 4. F 5. F

D 1. British partitioned Bengal with the hope that it would cause a rift between Hindus and Muslims.
2. Swadeshi movement was a part of the Indian national movement. It aimed at achieving the Indian independence by striking at the economic interests of the British Empire. It was an economic strategy which involved the boycott of foreign goods and use of home goods manufactured in India.
3. Satyagraha is a policy of passive political resistance against the British.
4. Gandhi marched to Dandi to oppose the salt tax.
5. Some of the important freedom fighters were Gandhi, Subhash Chandra Bose, Annie Besant.

Think

1. This is the Dandi March.
2. This happened during the Civil Disobedience Movement in 1930. This was done to break the salt law that the British had imposed on production of salt so as to control salt trade in India.

Life skills and values

Gandhiji's policy was better since British were one of the top imperial powers of the world with an unparalleled military strength. Indians may not have succeeded in warfare as was proved by the failure of the INA later on. Also, non-violence was a way to bring about masses of Indians into the struggle which till then had been dominated by the rich and elite only.

6 Indian Government

Take off

- Jawaharlal Nehru was the first prime minister of India.
- Narendra Modi is the current prime minister of India.

Warm up

Dr Rajendra Prasad

Do it yourself

Discipline*
Perseverance
Faith
Will
Knowledge
Good behaviour
Yes, these will help outside school as well.

Find out

Andhra Pradesh, Telangana, Bihar, Karnataka, Maharashtra and Uttar Pradesh have bicameral legislature.

Workout

A 1. a. 2. c. 3. a. 4. a. 5. a.

B 1. National government
2. Supreme Court
3. Speaker 4. President

C 1. T 2. F 3. T 4. F 5. T

D
1. The constitution of India provides the laws by which the country is supposed to be governed.
2. There are 28 states in India.
3. The highest judicial body of India is the Supreme Court.
4. The two houses of the Parliament are Lok Sabha and Rajya Sabha.
5. The central government looks after the union territories and president heads them.
6. The Central Government creates laws that are applicable for the whole country. This is done through the two houses of the parliament – Lok Sabha and Rajya Sabha.
7. The president is the head of the country. He is also the supreme commander of the armed forces. He or she is elected by the members of both the Houses of the Parliament as well as the state legislative assemblies. He serves a term of five years.
8. The elections are organized in all the 29 states of India in order to elect members of the state legislative assemblies. The state legislative assembly is also known as the Vidhan Sabha. The legislative assembly makes laws for the state. The members of these assemblies are called the members of legislative assembly (MLAs). They are elected for a term of five years.
   The political party that wins the election in a state is invited to create the state's government. The leader of this party is chosen as the chief minister, who in turn appoints a council of ministers to assist him or her. The head of a state is a governor. The president of India appoints the governors of the states.
9. The judiciary is also a part of the government. It ensures that all the citizens obey the laws. It provides justice and punishes those who have violated the laws of the country. It is made up of the different courts spread across the country. The members of the judiciary are called judges. All the states have a series of courts right from the lower courts to the High Courts. The High Court is the highest judicial authority in a state or a union territory. The districts in the state also have their own courts. The Supreme Court is the highest judicial body in India. It has the final say in all legal matters. The president of India appoints the judges of the High Courts and the Supreme Court.

Think

1. Parliament
2. This is where the laws are framed.

Life skills and values

1. State government
2. Central government
3. Courts
4. Central government

7 United Nations

Take off

- India lies in the continent of Asia.
- Countries of the world help each other when in need.

Warm up

United Nations

Find out

Kosovo, Taiwan or Republic of China, Abkhazia*

Do it yourself*

Kaziranga Wildlife Sanctuary, Assam
Manas Wildlife Sanctuary, Assam
Mahabodhi Temple Complex at Bodh Gaya, Bihar
Humayun's Tomb, Delhi
Qutb Minar and its monuments, Delhi

Red Fort Complex, Delhi
Churches and Convents of Goa
Champaner-Pavagadh Archaeological Park, Gujarat
Group of Monuments at Hampi
Group of Monuments at Pattadakal
Buddhist Monuments at Sanchi, Madhya Pradesh
Rock Shelters of Bhimbetka, Madhya Pradesh
Khajuraho Group of Monuments, Madhya Pradesh
Ajanta Caves
Ellora Caves
Elephanta Caves
Chhatrapati Shivaji Terminus
Sun Temple, Konark
Keoladeo National Park
Jantar Mantar, Jaipur
Great Living Chola Temples
Group of Monuments at Mahabalipuram
Agra Fort, Uttar Pradesh
Fatehpur Sikri, Uttar Pradesh
Taj Mahal, Uttar Pradesh
Mountain Railways of India
Nanda Devi and Valley of Flowers National Parks
Sundarbans National Park
Western Ghats
Hill Forts of Rajasthan
Rani ka Vav, Gujarat
Great Himalayan National Park

Workout

A 1. c. 2. c. 3. b. 4. c.

B 1. WHO
2. General Assembly
3. Secretary-General

C 1. T 2. F 3. T 4. F

D 1. The UN was formed to ensure global peace.
2. The objective of the UN is to maintain global peace through cordial relations between countries and work together to fight global problems and also help countries achieve their aims.
3. UNICEF looks after the welfare of children.
4. ICJ deals with international legal issues.
5. The work of the UN is carried out by six main organs. They are the General Assembly, Security Council, Economic and Social Council, Trusteeship Council, International Court of Justice and the Secretariat.
The General Assembly is the main body of the UN. It is like the parliament of the UN. All the member countries of the UN have one vote in the General Assembly. The Security Council maintains global peace and security. It has 15 members. UK, China, France, Russia and USA are its permanent members and the remaining are non-permanent members who are chosen for a term of two years. The Economic and Social Council looks after the economic, humanitarian, social and cultural activities that the UN undertakes. It has 54 member countries, which are elected to serve a term of 3 years. When the United Nations was created, there were 11 nations that required supervision. The Trusteeship Council was created to look after these nations. Today, this council is not functional anymore. The International Court of Justice is the legal court of the UN. It is located at The Hague in Netherlands. It deals with international legal issues and advises countries on international legal matters. The Secretariat deals with the daily activities of the UN. The Secretary General of the UN heads the Secretariat.
The UN also has some special agencies where it employs experts from the various fields of life in order to help its member nations. Some of them are listed below:
   - United Nations Educational, Scientific and Cultural Organization (UNESCO) encourages cooperation amongst countries and enables the exchange of information
   in the fields of education, science, culture and communication.
   - United Nations Children's Fund (UNICEF) defends, promotes and protects children's rights.
   - World Health Organization (WHO) manages international health work and conducts research on the cure, prevention and elimination of diseases.
   - Food and Agricultural Organization (FAO) works to eliminate hunger and malnutrition, and to raise the levels of nutrition.
   - International Labour Organization (ILO) formulates policies that ensure basic human rights for workers, improve their working as well as living conditions, and create more employment opportunities.
6. India became a member of the UN on 30 October 1945. As one of the founding members, India strongly supports the purposes and programmes of the UN. It has made significant contributions in the United

Nations peacekeeping missions by sending troops, reinforcements and conducting relief operations in war-struck areas and areas hit by calamities. In addition to all this, India is also one of the top contributors to the UN's regular budget. India, currently seeking permanent membership, has been elected as the member of the UN Security Council for seven terms.

7. The Trusteeship Council was set up as one of the main organs of the United Nations to help nations which were affected during the world war II.
8. United Nations Educational, Scientific and Cultural Organization (UNESCO) encourages cooperation amongst countries and enables the exchange of information in the fields of education, science, culture and communication. United Nations Children's Fund (UNICEF) defends, promotes and protects children's rights. World Health Organization (WHO) manages international health work and conducts research on the cure, prevention and elimination of diseases. Food and Agricultural Organization (FAO) works to eliminate hunger and malnutrition, and to raise the levels of nutrition. International Labour Organization (ILO) formulates policies that ensure basic human rights for workers, improve their working as well as living conditions, and create more employment opportunities.

Think

1. António Guterres
2. United Kingdom

Life skills and values

1. UNICEF
2. ILO
3. WHO
4. UNICEF

Review Corner

A 1. Fertilizers; 2. Chlorofluorocarbons; 3. magma; 4. Grand Trunk Road; 5. mass communication; 6. The Gateway of India; 7. radicals; 8.1942; 9. Five years; 10. Birsa Munda

B 1. True; 2. False; 3. False; 4. True; 5. True

C
1. Smoke from factories as it causes air pollution and not noise pollution.
2. The secretariat is not an organ of the UN
3. Waterways as it is used for travel by water and the other three on land.
4. Hume as he was not an Indian freedom fighter.
5. President as the president is not a member of any of the houses.

D 1. video call; 2. conserving; 3. cyclones; 4. Ramayana; 5. Raja Ram Mohan Roy

E
1. British territorial aggression and their new policies like land revenue rules, introduction of railways and telegraphs only led to discontent among the Indians who thought these to be interference in their lives. Dalhousie's policy of doctrine of lapse by which many Indian rulers were deposed also led them to band together to fight the British*
2. A proponent of civil rights, women's emancipation, and anti-imperialistic ideas, she was an important figure in India's struggle for independence from colonial rule.
3. The judiciary is also a part of the government. It ensures that all the citizens obey the laws. It provides justice and punishes those who have violated the laws of the country. It is made up of the different courts spread across the country. The members of the judiciary are called judges. All the states have a series of courts right from the lower courts to the High Courts. The High Court is the highest judicial authority in a state or a union territory. The districts in the state also have their own courts. The Supreme Court is the highest judicial body in India. It has the final say in all legal matters. The president of India appoints the judges of the High Courts and the Supreme Court.
4. The burning of fossil fuels, agricultural activities, exhaust from factories and industries, mining operations are some of the causes of air pollution.
5. One of the major reasons of a tsunami is an underwater volcanic eruption or undersea earthquake. The following precautions should be taken before a tsunami:
   - In case a tsunami warning has been given, we should immediately evacuate and get to higher ground.
   - The sea shores should be evacuated immediately.
   - People living in coastal areas should not go back to their homes until the authorities declare it to be safe.

Worksheet Answers

1 Environmental Pollution

A
1. Smoke and poisonous gases emitted from cars and factories, Garbage thrown into water bodies, Excessive honking and use of harmful chemicals like pesticides.
2. When harmful substances and gases increase in a place the temperature increases, affecting the climate and polluting air this depletes the ozone layer.
3. Use of harmful chemicals like fertilizers, improper disposal of waste in landfills and dumping plastic, glass and metal scraps.
4. Excessive honking by drivers, loud music and fire crackers.

B 1. d 2. e 3. a 4. c 5. b

C Students will do themselves.

D Students will do themselves.

2 Evolution of Transport and Communication

A
1. James Watt
2. Marconi
3. John Logie Baird
4. Samuel Morse
5. Alexander Graham

B 1. c 2. d 3. a 4. e 5. b

C 1. 1876 2. 1886 3. 1926 4. 1443 5. 1903

D
1. Early man began with each other through signs and hand gestures. They drew pictures on the walls of the caves.
2. Railways are an important means of transport, they connect different countries in Europe and north America. France and china have some of the fastest trains in the world.
3. Cinema is another audio-visual means of mass communication it helps in educating and entertaining people, it is informative.
4. People used to copy books by hand, it was time consuming process and it was very costly to produce these books.
5. Oil tankers were used for oil transport, cruise ships used for ferry passengers, refrigerated ships to transport vegetables, fruits and dairy products.

3 India Over the Ages

A
1. Britishers
2. Krishnadevaraya
3. Babur
4. Delhi Sultanate, Mughal
5. Magadha

B 1. d 2. e 3. b 4. c 5. a

C
1. Hampi, Vijayanagara Empire
2. Sanchi Stupa, Ashoka
3. Buland Darwaza, Akbar
4. Rashtrapati Bhavan, British
5. Red Fort, Shah Jahan

4 British Period in India

A 1. 1757 2. 1764 3. 1857 4. 1885

B 1. b 2. c 3. d 4. a

C
1. Dadabhai Naoroji, Badruddin Tyabji, Pherozeshah Mehta, Surendranath Banerjee and Gopal Krishna Gokhale
2. Child marriage, Female infanticide and sati
3. Trade between India and European countries like the Netherlands, France and Great Britain flourished and each country established trading companies in India What was the effect of the new sea route discovery?
4. The revolt was started by the Indian soldiers known as sepoys serving in British Army at Meerut.
5. The people understood that the Britishers were not interested in developing the nation

* These are suggested answers hence accept other valid answers too.

but only interested to accumulate wealth hence the Indian National Congress was formed to free India from the Britishers and have Purna Swaraj.

5 Attaining Freedom

A

1. Name the three reformers who revolted against the partition of Bengal.

   Bal Gangadhar Tilak, Lala Lajpat Rai and Bipin Chandra Pal.
2. The British feared the unity of Indians and decided to create a divide among them, The Partition of Bengal was devised to achieve this motive.
3. On 13 April 1919 thousands of people gathered at the Jallianwala Bagh in Amritsar for a peaceful protest. The Britishers blocked the exit and opened fire on the gathering killing many people.
4. In 1930 British introduced a salt tax on the production of salt in order to control salt trade. Gandhiji lad a march from Sabarmati ashram to Dandi with hundreds of people where he made salt in defiance of the British law.
5. Gandhiji assumed leadership of Indian National congress and led nationwide non-violent protests called satyagraha.

B

1. Divide and rule
2. Swadeshi movement
3. Satyagraha
4. Purna swaraj
5. Dandi March

C 1. 1930 2. 1905 3. 1885 4. 1947 5. 1919

D Bal Gangadhar Tilak, Lala Lajpat Rai and Bipin Chandra Pal encouraged the people of India to protest the partition of Bengal. The were the flagbearers of the Swadeshi movement.

6 Indian Government

A

1. The Constitution
2. The Central Government.
3. The legislature makes Laws
4. The Lok Sabha
5. Speaker

B 1. e 2. c 3. d 4. b 5. a

C

1. Governor
2. Chief minister
3. President
4. Vice President
5. Speaker

7 United Nations

A

1. Six
2. Peace
3. Trygve Lie
4. Hague in Netherlands
5. Secretariat

B

1. United Nations Educational Scientific and Cultural Organization
2. World Health Organization
3. United Nations Children's Fund
4. International Labour Organization
5. Food and Agricultural Organization

C

1. It maintains global peace and security, it has 15 members, 5 are permanent members, if there is a mis understanding, conflict or disputes among member countries the security council resolves them.
2. The membership to the Un is open to all peace-loving states that are willing to accept the terms given in the charter.
3. It has 54-member countries who are elected to serve a term period of 3 years. It has a chain of agencies spread across the world, which work on different social crises human rights issues and many more.
4. FAO works to eliminate hunger and malnutrition, and to raise the levels of nutrition.
5. India became a member of the UN on 30 October 1945. As one of the founding members, India strongly supports the purposes and programmes of the UN. It has made significant contributions in the United Nations peacekeeping missions by sending troops, reinforcements and conducting relief operations in war-struck areas and areas hit by calamities.

Workbook Answers

1 Environmental Pollution

Worksheet

1. Carbon Dioxide; 2. Dodo; 3. Panda bears; 4. Sunlight; 5. vegetable peels.

2 Evolution of Transport and Communication

Worksheet

1. James Watt; 2. France to Turkey; 3. China; 4. Seikan; 5. Asia and Europe.

3 India Over the Ages

A 1. Ancient; 2. Medieval; 3. Ancient; 4. Modern

B The Mamluk/Slave dynasty (1206–1290), the Khilji dynasty (1290–1320), the Tughlaq dynasty (1320–1414), the Sayyid dynasty (1414–1451), and the Lodi dynasty (1451–1526).

4 British Period in India

Worksheet

A 1498 – D; 1757 – E; 1764 – A; 1857 – C; 1885 – B

B 1. a 2. b 3. c

5 Attaining Freedom

Worksheet

A 1. Dr. Rajendra Prasad; 2. Subhas Chandra Bose

B Across – 3.apartheid; 6. Malpractice

Down – 1. suppress; 2. Non-violent; 4. partition; 5. defiance; 7. protest

6 Indian Government

Worksheet

A

P	A	R	L	I	A	M	E	N	T	T	R	P	V	J
I	Q	R	H	X	M	I	R	O	N	Y	R	G	I	U
L	S	D	U	E	E	E	F	E	T	I	N	S	D	D
O	Q	L	S	T	S	C	M	S	M	G	C	L	H	I
K	E	L	O	I	A	A	U	E	E	E	V	D	A	C
S	T	S	P	E	A	K	E	R	Y	Q	S	U	N	I
A	U	E	A	L	J	I	S	R	I	V	Q	G	S	A
B	N	L	E	G	I	S	L	A	T	U	R	E	A	R
H	R	A	P	R	E	S	I	D	E	N	T	A	B	Y
A	P	Q	S	T	E	S	D	I	L	E	B	S	H	X
S	L	T	B	L	S	A	A	W	X	J	L	P	A	S
A	E	R	A	J	Y	A	S	A	B	H	A	J	Y	A
R	S	U	P	R	E	M	E	C	O	U	R	T	D	S
Q	R	E	X	E	C	U	T	I	V	E	R	Q	X	J
P	R	I	M	E	M	I	N	I	S	T	E	R	J	X

B 1. central; 2. state; 3. Speaker; 4. Vidhan; 5.

7 United Nations

Worksheet

1. Agra Fort; 2. Hill Forts of Rajasthan; 3. Fatehpur Sikri; 4. Buddhist Monuments at Sanchi; 5. Khajuraho Group of Monuments; 6. Great Himalayan National Park Conservation Area; 7. Rock Shelters of Bhimbetka; 8. Mahabodhi Temple Complex at Bodh Gaya; 9. Group of Monuments at Hampi.

Review Corner

A 1. b; 2. c; 3. b; 4. b; 5. c

B 1. false; 2. true; 3. false; 4. true; 5. true

C
1. Equatorial; it is not a classification of a climatic zone
2. Ranches are farmlands and not grasslands
3. A letter is a media of personal communication and not mass communication
4. Hume; he is not an Indian freedom fighter
5. Swiss; they did not have trade relations with India.

D
1. Factors affecting the climate of a place are: (i) Latitude of a place and the tilt of the Earth determines the amount of sunlight it receives. (ii) Altitude of a place or its height from sea level also has an effect on the climatic pattern of the place. Normally, hilly areas have a cooler climate than the plains. As the height increases, the air becomes thinner, resulting in a moderate

climate. (iii) Distance from the sea is another important factor that determines the climate of a place. Oceans and seas regulate the climate of areas around them by absorbing the sun's heat. (iv) Humidity, the extent of moisture present in the air, influences the climate. The areas near the equator have high humidity, hence they experience hot and humid climate. (v) The types and the direction of wind also affect the climate of a place. Different types of winds—hot, cold, humid and dry—have different effects on the climate.

2. The vegetation in the temperate grasslands primarily includes tall and short grasses. Tall grasses grow in areas that receive heavy rainfall, while short grasses grow in areas that have a continental climate. During autumn, the grasses wither and turn into hay. A few trees grow along the coasts in the southern temperate grasslands.

3. Communication can be categorized into two types: (i) Personal communication normally takes place between two people—the receiver and the sender. Letters, telegraph, telephone, fax and e-mail are a few examples of personal communication. (ii) Mass communication takes place when something is communicated to a large number of people. This is done through newspapers, magazines, radio, television, Internet, cinema and advertisements.

4. The English-educated Indians were influenced by modern thoughts and ideas, which were spread through articles in various English and regional newspapers. The growth of railways helped to bring the people of the country closer. Feelings of nationalism and patriotism arose amongst the Indians. The educated Indians worked towards social reforms. Reformers like Raja Rammohan Roy, Ishwar Chandra Vidyasagar, Maharshi Debendranath Tagore and Dayanand Saraswati all raised their voices against various social evils like child marriage, caste system, female infanticide and sati. They also encouraged education for women and were in favour of widow remarriage.

5. Mohandas Karamchand Gandhi, also known as the Father of the Nation, was born on 2 October 1869 in Gujarat. He was one of India's greatest freedom fighters. He taught people that independence could be achieved by non-violent and peaceful means. Gandhi had initially spent a few years in South Africa and there he contributed in the struggle against apartheid using non-violence and Satyagraha. When he came back to India, he was shocked to see extensive poverty in India. He decided to use the same methods he used in South Africa to help India gain independence. This marked the beginning of the Satyagraha movement. He protested against several social and religious malpractices in India and also asked people not to obey the laws that were unjust. Peaceful protests and marches were held all around the country even though the protestors were often badly beaten.